Your Child at Play: Two to Three Years

Your Child at Play: Two to Three Years

Dr. Marilyn Segal
and
Dr. Don Adcock

Yvonne Koves

Newmarket Press
New York

In memory of my father, A. L. Mailman,
lover of children and master of child play.

First Edition
1 2 3 4 5 6 7 8 9 0   F/C
1 2 3 4 5 6 7 8 9 0   F/P

Library of Congress Cataloging in Publication Data

Segal, Marilyn M.
    Your child at play: two to three years.

    Bibliography: p.
    Includes index.
    1. Child development.   2. Child rearing.   3. Play.
4. Learning.   I. Adcock, Don.   II. Title.
HQ767.9.S43   1985   649′.122   84-12598
ISBN 0-937858-54-4
ISBN 0-937858-55-2 (pbk.)

The authors gratefully acknowledge the continuing grant from the A. L. Mailman
Family Foundation, Inc., which supported the writing of this book.
A special thank you to Monica Segal for her careful and creative editing, and to
Patti Lieberman for her persistent bird-dogging of all our revisions and additions.

Volumes in the *Your Child at Play* series:
    Your Child at Play: Birth to One Year
    Your Child at Play: One to Two Years
    Your Child at Play: Two to Three Years
Published simultaneously in hardcover and paperback editions

Quantity Purchases
Companies, professional groups, clubs, and other organizations may qualify for special
terms when ordering quantities of this title. For information, contact the Special Sales
Department, Newmarket Press, 3 East 48th Street, New York, New York 10017. Phone
(212) 832-3575.

Manufactured in the United States of America

TABLE OF CONTENTS

INTRODUCTION

"Do you want to know about our Emily? Well, she does everything two-year olds are supposed to do. She stamps, pouts, bites, whines, pulls the dog's tail and colors on the wall paper. She's stubborn, pesty, exasperating, captivating and adorable. As a matter of fact, she's like New England weather. If you don't like what's going on — wait a minute."

This thumb-nail description of a two-year old, provided by a doting father, captures some of the salient qualities of two-year old behavior. Between two and three years of age, children are making dramatic strides in every facet of development. Their language is growing in leaps and bounds, play is becoming more imaginative and new social skills are emerging. As two-year olds demonstrate new capabilities, the family's expectations increase. Quite naturally, there are times when a child and a family are out of phase. When the family is expecting grown-up behavior, the two-year old wants to be a baby. When the family is expecting compliant behavior, the two-year old wants to be the boss.

Two to Three Years is a book about everyday living with a two-year old. It is the third volume of a trilogy that traces the development of young children from birth to three years old. Like the other volumes in the series, *Two to Three Years* is based on a study of approximately one hundred families who were visited both at home and in The Family Center. A primary purpose of the book is to help parents understand the developmental changes that are taking place, and to know what will happen next. Although we do not believe that there is only one way to raise a child, we do not steer away from giving advice on child rearing. Throughout this book we talk about routine problems that are a part of living with two-year olds, and we describe some of the creative ways parents have found to cope with these everyday problems.

One reason, then, for writing this book is to share ideas on child rearing. A second reason is to provide the reader with a sampling of two year old behavior. When two-year olds demonstrate behavior that is difficult or puzzling, it is important for parents to see this behavior in perspective. Is the child's behavior really out of the ordinary, or has the same scene been enacted time and time again in other homes with other two-year olds? A third reason for writing this book is to increase the pleasure that parents receive from their children. As parents are sensitized to the developmental leaps that the two-year old is making, the bad moments are easier to cope with and the good moments are all the more marvelous.

In order to emphasize the personal experiences that parents and children share, we have included many anecdotes in this book. These incidents fit within the pattern of typical development, while at the same time illustrating the unique qualities of real children. Each parent-child relationship described in this book has its own distinctive character.

Young children are often intensely single-minded. A child may want to hear the same story over and over, play out the same pretend theme, or spend hours outside investigating the backyard. Intensity is a characteristic of parents as well. At times we become single-mindedly involved in teaching our children some new skill—how to put on shoes,how to enjoy reading, how to swing a bat.

For better or worse, this intensity is the most prominent characteristic of the daily interaction between young children and parents. There may be strong conflict if the energies of parents and children are concentrated on different activities. But when these activities are united in a common rhythm, there is mutually satisfying sharing. Whenever possible, we have tried to capture the flavor of this intensity in our examples.

Our intimate involvement with the parents and children described in this book has been a rewarding experience. Our belief in the untapped potential of young children and our conviction that parents can tap this potential have been confirmed. Each questionnaire that we read and each home visit we made have given us new ideas and provided us with new insights. We would like, through this text, to share our sense of discovery with the reader.

Chapter 1
GROWING UP:
AN OVERVIEW

We asked parents of two-year olds to tell us what they enjoyed most about their children. The answers they gave were illuminating:

> The most enjoyable experience I have had is communication with my child: being able to communicate more and more one to the other.

> We made a visit to the Miami Seaquarium. Kim was fascinated with the fish exhibits and the whale show. It was such a pleasure watching her learn new things.

> When we visited Matthew's great grandmother, who is ninety-one years old, Matthew showed a particular kindness for her. As we left to get into the car, he let go of my hand, looked up at her and said, "A kiss, a hug!"

The "terrible twos," according to the reports of the parents we visited, are not as troublesome as the label implies. Living with a two-year old is de-

manding, but it also is rewarding. In this book we will examine life with a two-year old in great detail. We will discuss the child rearing options available to parents. We will also describe how two-year olds make friends, learn language, develop pretend themes, and continue to explore their environment. In this introductory chapter we will focus on the broad world view that evolves between two and three years of age.

Two-year olds experience rapid intellectual growth and emotional change. A major outcome of this growth is a new capacity to recognize themselves as separate individuals. Children become increasingly aware of their power to affect other people, especially parents, and they develop a distinctive style for social interaction. At the same time, they soak up new information and begin to realize the vastness of the world. Their vision of time and space, of life itself, expands tremendously. We will discuss the emerging world view of two-year olds in terms of these two perspectives, a new sense of self and the making of new discoveries.

A New Sense of Self

Self-Recognition

By the age of two, many children can recognize their own photograph. They certainly recognize their own image in a mirror. They already have discovered, or are on the verge of discovering, their sexual identity, and they generally are aware that human bodies consist of standard parts. In short, the children have a superficial, but stable, sense of their physical selves.

This physical sense of self does not exist in a vacuum. It is embedded in a larger environment of material things and, like other people, two-year olds support their sense of identity by laying claim to this larger world. Being less sure of themselves, their possessiveness is more rigid and shrill. "That's mine," becomes a pronouncement with virtually no limits. Two-year olds are possessive about their toys, their clothes, their house, even their parents.

For a two-year old, possessions are a way of extending a primitive sense of self. They provide stability rather than status. Several parents told us their children reacted negatively when the family car was traded in for a new one. The new car was fancier, but the old car was familiar. Moving to a new house, or even changing the furniture in the old house, was upsetting to some children. "I don't want you to take down my crib," Matthew insisted, even though he hadn't slept in his crib for months. "I don't want new shoes," Heather screamed, holding on desperately to a wrapped pair of sneakers.

Two year old children also are beginning to appreciate the existence of their inner selves, although it will be several years before they realize that

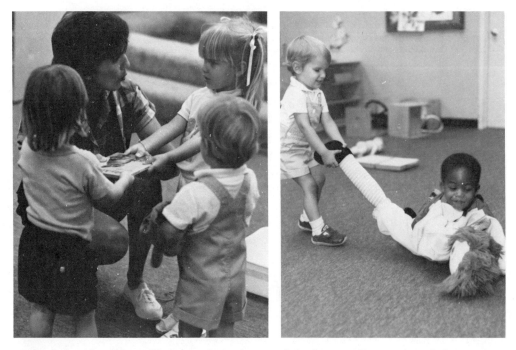

each individual has distinct thoughts and feelings. One sign of this growing awareness is an interest in identifying preferences. The children go beyond the immediate feeling of "I want" or "I don't want" and focus on "I like"
or "I don't like." "I want that," Kori said to her Nana as she pointed to some
iced coffee. "You won't like it," Nana explained. "It has a bitter taste." "I want
to try that," Kori insisted a little more firmly. "Okay, try it," Nana agreed. "Take
a little taste." Kori tried it. "I don't like Nana's coffee. I like Daddy's tea
better."

Another sign of increased self-awareness is the growing ability of two-
year olds to talk about their emotions. "It's a beautiful day," Zachary exclaimed joyfully as he and his mother chased a butterfly across the backyard. "I swinging, I swinging, I swinging, I so happy swinging," sang Wendy
as she swung higher and higher at the park. On the negative side, Eddie
let his father know how he felt about not being allowed to play with the toaster.
"I hate you bad," he shouted emphatically. Jodi ran into her mother's room
after watching a scary television show. "Mommy, that T.V. makes my tummy
shake."

Two-year olds are not only more articulate about their own feelings, they
show greater sensitivity toward the feelings of others. When Allison acci-
dentally broke a vase, she asked her mother plaintively, "Are you sad?" Janet, who was just gaining enough control to use the toilet, greeted her mother
at the door. "Feel my pants, Mommy. Are you happy?"

Self-Assertion

The self-awareness of two-year olds comes out, above all, in the form of self-assertion. Assertive techniques include screaming, arguing, rationalizing, threatening, ordering, teasing, whining, hitting, kissing, hugging, making cute faces, and many others. Although these assertive techniques sometimes appear to be negative developments, they indicate social growth. Children from two to three concentrate on exploring their social environment, just as they focused earlier on the physical environment. The outcome of these explorations is a new repertoire of social skills.

A critical task for two-year olds is learning when and how to use their new social skills. It is a problem of discrimination. Each technique has its place and is acceptable at times. The fact that parents respond differently in different situations makes it more difficult for children to learn how to behave. In reality, social interaction is very complicated. It is not governed by a set of straightforward and simplistic rules.

For children who have just turned two, the most prominent technique for self-assertion is likely to be a defiant "no." Children discover that a "no" has power, and they use it at every opportunity.

> Mother: "Tommy, would you like to come to the drugstore with Daddy and me?"
>
> Tommy: "No, don't wanna."
>
> Mother: "You can pick out a birthday card to send to Pop-Pop."
>
> Tommy: "No, don't wanna."
>
> Mother: "Okay, then stay here with Jeffrey."
>
> Tommy: (Bursting into tears.) "Me go drugstore, Mommy, Daddy."

Verbal forms of resistance become more subtle as the language ability of a two-year old increases. Kori, for example, developed a string of imaginary characters who provided a ready-made excuse for resisting parental requests. "Would you like to help me put away your toys so that we'll be ready to go out when Daddy comes?" her mother asked. "No, I can't," Kori explained. "I have to look after Aki and her sisters and all the little babies." Amy, who discovered that she got special consideration because of a headache, started to develop stomach aches, leg aches, and back aches. Even peas were refused at dinner because "they hurt my mouth."

Conversely, two-year olds develop positive techniques for manipulating parents. A "please," a hug, a kiss, or a little flattery go a long way toward keeping parents "in line." Heather, for example, gave her father lots of hugs and kisses when he did things her way. When her father "misbehaved," she let him give her a goodnight kiss and then wiped it away with her sheet. Jenny varied her technique to fit the situation. When she wanted candy from Grandma, she asked in a polite voice, "Please, Baba, candy." When she wanted a story from Daddy, she cuddled up on his lap and gave him a hug. A particularly effective strategy that some two-year olds learn is "I'm sorry." Shawn had been playing with the water pump, although he knew full well that it was off limits. Just as his mother was about to scold him, Shawn looked up with a most innocent expression. "I sorry. You angry, Mommy?"

Two-year olds practice new social skills just like any other new skill they develop. It would be incorrect, however, to assume that children are only involved in testing their ability to manipulate parents. When two year old children assert themselves, regardless of the technique, there usually is some genuine emotion involved.

Pamela's family told us they could not stand Pamela's incessant whining. Sure enough, as soon as we got to the house, Pamela began whining for a cookie. Her mother explained that she could not have a cookie because it was too close to lunch. Pamela continued to whine. Finally her mother could not hold out any more and gave Pamela a piece of cookie.

In this particular incident it was quite clear that Pamela's mother had reinforced the whining behavior. Pamela had learned from this incident, and probably from a lot more like it, that if your first whine does not produce the

desired result, you had better whine louder and longer.

This example suggests that parents should never give in to whining. Such a rule, however, would overlook the fact that children whine because they are sad. Pamela was genuinely unhappy because she could not understand the reason for prohibiting cookies before lunch. In this instance it would have been better for Pamela's mother to resist her request, but what if Pamela had been whining for some nutritious snack or because another child had taken away her toy? In these cases many parents would decide that a child's unhappy feelings outweighed the manipulative aspects of whining. The parents might ask the children to make their requests in a different tone of voice, but they would not deny the requests because of whining.

Temper tantrums are an even more disconcerting form of self-assertion. Timothy's mother told us about a recent tantrum that had occurred at a park. Like many two-year olds, Timothy loved exploring the playground equipment at parks. As a special treat they had stopped at a new park on their way downtown. After fifteen or twenty minutes, his mother said it was time to leave and go shopping. His response was, "I don't wanna." When she took his hand, he suddenly pulled away, threw himself on the ground, and started to scream. "That tantrum really wasn't too bad," Timothy's mother remarked. "Nobody else was near us, so I didn't feel embarrassed. I ignored Timothy's screaming, just picked him up and put him in the car. But when he pulls that kind of trick in a grocery store or restaurant, I don't know what to do."

As in Pamela's whining, there was both manipulation and genuine emotion in Timothy's behavior. He had learned from previous experience that he sometimes got his way by screaming. At the same time, he was genuinely angry because he could not understand the need to leave the park. Again, we have selected an example in which most parents would not respond to the temper tantrum. But what if Timothy had lost his temper because he could not complete a puzzle or because his ice cream cone had fallen on the ground? In such situations, many parents would respond to the child's expression of frustration and rage. They would offer to help with the puzzle or they would buy another ice cream cone. Each situation is different. Sometimes we refuse to be manipulated, sometimes we respond to the child's feelings, and sometimes we search for a compromise. There are no standard answers.

Feelings of Ambivalence

Each two-year old blends different social skills into a personal style. Some children excel in being argumentative and defiant. Some are especially good at manipulating parents with hugs and kisses. Some make excuses and invent imaginary scapegoats. Some are whiners. All are struggling with feelings of ambivalence about growing up.

"Now I am a boy," Matthew told his mother as he pulled on a new pair of underpants. "Now I am a baby," he announced later as his naptime diaper was put on. The transition from babyhood to childhood is not accomplished without detours and backtracking. One moment the two-year old refuses his father's hand as he mounts a flight of stairs or walks along a busy street. A moment later he is afraid of stepping over a crack in the sidewalk and asks his father to carry him. Two-year olds want to do things for themselves but at the same time find it difficult to give up the protective environment of babyhood.

The brunt of this ambivalence will be directed toward parents and it is not unusual to see a complete change in children's behavior when parents are not around. Similar stories are recounted about first visits with relatives: the children acted like perfect angels, no hassles, no temper tantrums, and no defiance. From the moment the children got home, however, the spell of good behavior came to an abrupt halt. Parents described the children as being downright stubborn, reverting to babyish behavior, whining, asking to be carried, and even demanding a bottle. "Grandma just spoiled her rotten," one mother complained.

Although Grandma may have broad shoulders, it is probably not accurate

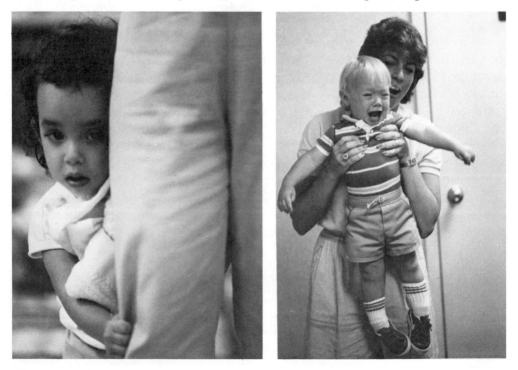

to describe this reversion to babyishness as a reaction to spoiling. More likely the child is demonstrating a normal reaction to a temporary loss of home. Being on their best behavior with relatives and coping with a new environment is a strain for two-year olds. When they return home, they feel secure enough to release pent-up feelings of ambivalence and to abandon their grown-up posture. Two-year olds do look forward to outings with adults other than their parents and they develop special relationships with grandparents, aunts and uncles, and teachers. Despite these expanding social horizons, however, parents continue to serve as the base of security for the two-year old. Two-year olds may have a marvelous time exploring new relationships but, in an emotional sense, they do not stray far from home.

New Discoveries

Space and Time

A fundamental insight during the period of infancy is that objects have permanence. Rattles, bottles and people continue to exist even if they can't be seen or touched. At two years old, children develop a new appreciation of the world's permanence. Space and time extend beyond the boundaries of their immediate experience.

An awareness of far-away places is seen in different ways. Two-year olds may be curious about people who get on planes and disappear into the sky, or they may note that the sun seems to sink into some distant hole at night. Perhaps they dimly realize that certain relatives live in a different part of the world, or that some unusual animal, such as a shark, lives far out in the ocean. Heath and Colby yelled "Grandma" everytime they saw the "Wild Kingdom" on television. Grandma was not part of the "Wild Kingdom" but she did live in Omaha, and the twins knew that the program was sponsored by a far-away building called Mutual of Omaha.

Just as two-year olds expand their vision of space, so do they extend their sense of time. "I rode a horse last night," Melissa told us. "She means the merry-go-round at the carnival," her mother explained, "and it wasn't really last night, it was a couple of weeks ago." Although her sense of time was not very precise, Melissa had made a critical distinction. She was able to indicate that the horse ride had not been a part of the current day's events.

Two-year olds also begin to anticipate future events. Helaine loved to go to the bowling alley with her mother on Thursdays. The first thing she asked every morning was, "Is it bowling day?" Helaine had learned to think of time in terms of days, and since bowling occurred regularly, she hoped that each day would be the special one. Michael had progressed further. He had linked two days together. On Tuesday nights, Michael's mother went to a class and a baby sitter stayed with Michael. On Wednesdays, he went to a play group. Rather than asking every morning about Shawn, his friend at playgroup, Michel instead waited until the morning after the baby sitter. He had learned that first came the baby sitter and then came Shawn.

The time words that two-year olds use reflect their limited conceptual framework. Melissa was not necessarily confused when she described an experience several weeks in the past as "last night." She used "last night" to refer to any past event. Lacking a system for combining days into weeks, she found an alternative. Things happen either today, a day in the past, or a day in the future, for which Melissa used "in a couple days." Other children use "yesterday" and "tomorrow" as their all-purpose terms.

The appearance of these terms makes it possible for two-year olds to talk about time. In turn, parents find it much easier to talk to the children about the past and the future. However, these terms represent new concepts that are just emerging and it is not essential that two-year olds use them. Even without special words for the past and future, children will be learning to organize time into larger and larger units.

New Number Concepts

Ultimately the organization of space and time depends on number concepts. Space and time are quantified in phrases such as "three miles away" and "ten minutes ago." Although two-year olds may pick up a random phrase

here and there, the application of numbers to space and time is beyond them. However, awareness of number concepts is beginning in other ways.

Numbers are mentioned most frequently in connection with age. Children learn to hold up two fingers when asked how old they are, or three if they want to indulge in a bit of wishful thinking. It will be a long time, however, before the children understand that they are talking about two years.

Although children do not grasp the meaning of two years, they may understand the idea of two fingers. Fingerplays and other informal games help establish the "twoness" of the human body—two eyes, two ears, two hands, two feet. Pairing objects is almost an instinct with people and two-year olds are no exception. Carrying one object in the right hand and another in the left hand is a natural way to make two. Jason surprised his parents one day by placing two hair brushes on the floor and announcing "two." Soon afterwards he found two shoes to carry, two tooth brushes, two trucks.

Recognizing two is more of a visual accomplishment than an act of counting. Two year old children may learn to recognize other visual numbers in the same way, such as five fingers on a hand or four wheels on a car. There is a mathematical regularity in any environment that can be recognized visually if encouraged by parents.

In addition to recognizing certain quantities, many two-year olds begin to count. Gillian was attracted to the animated counting sequences on "Sesame Street." The machine gun rhythm, which Gillian's parents found nerve-racking, invariably caught her attention. When her father introduced the idea of counting the buttons on a new dress, Gillian responded enthusiastically.

Traditionally, the fun of counting was emphasized by rhymes such as "one, two, buckle my shoe." "Sesame Street" has shown us an even more powerful technique: shout and count. Parents have become more concerned with teaching children to count and, because of the razzle-dazzle on television, counting has become an enjoyable social activity. In addition, there are a number of excellent books that are designed to introduce counting to young children.

This early counting tends to be rote; that is, it is a language exercise in which children merely repeat number words in the proper sequence. Rote counting is not necessarily accurate. A child may skip some objects while counting others more than once. Even the rote sequence may be confused. Jason started with five instead of one. Gillian always left out seven.

With practice and assistance, some two year old children can learn to count accurately. Donald's mother helped him touch each picture in a counting book as they counted out loud together. Beverly's mother had taught her to pick up each object and move it when counting, so that no object would be missed or double-counted.

The transition from rote to rational counting is not an instantaneous process. For many young children, the two coexist, with rational counting being used when a small quantity is involved and rote counting taking over when a quantity becomes too large. Barbara, for example, had learned to count the four people in her family and she could count four objects in other situations too. However, when she tried to count the presents under the Christmas tree, her deliberate counting style disappeared. She touched the packages and cheerfully recited various number sequences, as if playing a private counting game.

The range of a two-year old's counting skills is not very important. The difference between being able to count to three versus ten is not going to matter in the years ahead. The significance of this new concept is that children are becoming aware of quantity. They are beginning to realize that there is a systematic method for counting objects, whether they come in a big bunch, a small bunch, or one at a time.

New Ideas About Life

New concepts of space, time and number help two-year olds make the world more predictable and permanent. They provide a better framework for making new discoveries of all kinds. Two year old children explore a great variety of new ideas, and each child's focus of interest is different. The one common link which exists between these interests is the idea of life.

Two-year olds are beginning to appreciate the special qualities of living things. Enhanced by the impressive noises they make, trucks, buses and other machines may seem to be alive. Above all, two-year olds are attracted to

animals as another form of life, attracted and yet apprehensive, too, for animals are both exciting and frightening.

The animals two-year olds know best are family pets. A family pet is accepted as a member of the family, and two-year olds develop a special relationship with this "brother" or "sister." For one thing, the pet has the fewest privileges in the family. All sorts of restrictions are placed on its behavior, and the two-year old is the first one to enforce these special rules. "Mittens, you bad boy," scolded Jodi. "You get off the table." Chris took even greater delight when "Pooh" jumped on a visitor's lap. "Dad," he reported excitedly, "Pooh is bugging our company."

Without question, the two-year old's style is to boss or control the family pet. The primary means of controlling a pet is to handle it: to pet and poke it, to hug and kiss it, to carry it around. Yet behind this bossiness is a desire to make friends, to form a personal relationship with the pet. Laura insisted on taking her dog into the bathroom with her. Jason cried when the cat would not sit next to him and watch television.

Because young children try so hard to make friends with family pets, parents often find themselves explaining the need to be gentle. Being too rough with a pet may hurt it. On the other hand, the animal can hurt the child by biting or scratching. These are difficult concepts for a child to understand and they cannot be learned without trial and error. During the time the child is experimenting with ways to handle animals, it is best if the family pet is even-tempered and robust.

Two-year olds also are interested in extending their animal friendships. Birds are among the most common animals in any environment, and it is not unusual for a two-year old to chase a duck or pigeon. Although the child

enjoys the chase, the real object is to catch, or at least touch, the bird and make friends. Feeding an animal is another way to make contact, and children's petting zoos are ideal for this purpose.

Despite the fact that two-year olds enjoy touching and feeding a variety of animals, there still is a strong element of fear associated with them. Kori, who was familiar with the family dog, was reluctant to pet her cousin Jennifer's cat. "Why don't you help Jennifer pet Isaac?" Jennifer's mother suggested to Kori. "I really don't think I should," Kori rationalized. "I have a cold."

One way to relate to animals without taking any chances is through an imaginative experience. Even two-year olds who have little opportunity to meet real animals, or who are afraid of real animals, enjoy listening to an animal story. Usually these animals are personified. They talk, wear clothes and eat human food. These stories may not provide much factual information about animals, but they reinforce a young child's desire to identify with other forms of life.

From time to time, two-year olds comment on differences between people and animals. Most often they will point out, in a disappointed tone of voice, that animals cannot really talk. Some children notice that animals do not use toilets and that many of them do not have hands. These distinctions only serve to highlight the strong affinity that young children have for animals.

It seems to us that parents play an essential role in helping two-year olds relate to animals. The children are drawn to the variety of animal life around them, and it is an appropriate time for parents to encourage a respect for life. Of all the families we visited, Benjie's and Jamie's parents expressed this feeling most clearly. During our visit, Benjie found a bug outside and, with a loud cry, he smashed it. His mother reminded him that he was not supposed to kill a bug until after he had asked his parents if it was a good bug or a bad bug. Jamie, Benjie's three year old brother, knew that spiders were "good bugs." Recently he had found several dead spiders in the house and commented, "Daddy's spiders are dead." On another occasion, Benjie and Jamie had collected some snails in a can. Their father noticed one of the snails crawling out of the can and said to the boys, "Look, the snail is trying to go home." He persuaded Benjie and Jamie to put the can on the porch so all the snails could go home, and by the next morning they were gone.

Just as two-year olds are beginning to recognize a wider range of life, they also are becoming more aware of the life process itself. They are most aware that animals, including people, move and eat. In addition, they sometimes are exposed to the idea that life is a process of renewal, of birth and death. Questions about birth and death are inspired by direct experience. Jodi, for example, was very curious about the new baby born in her family, and was verbal enough to put her puzzlement into words: "Mommy, did I drink from your nipples when I was a baby? What did I do when I was inside you?"

Questions about death are less common because families try to shield children from this fact of life. When a death does occur in the immediate family, however, some two-year olds pursue the subject. After the death of

his grandmother, Jed asked over and over again when they were going to get Grandma back. His mother explained what had happened, but the questions continued. Finally, she gave him a picture of his grandmother to keep by his bed, and he seemed to be satisfied. Daren, another two-year old, found his own method of coming to terms with a grandparent's death. He had asked no questions during the funeral, and his family took it for granted that he really wasn't aware of what was going on. Then his mother noticed that he was drawing intently on a small slate. "I making Grandpa," he said to himself as he made some circular squiggles. After several minutes, he picked up the eraser, rubbed the slate vigorously, and continued with his monologue. "Where Grandpa go?—Grandpa all gone!"

As two-year olds gain new insights into themselves and other people, and as they experience the whole range of human emotions, they are forming a sense of themselves as individual people. They also are developing a set of expectations about the world and the people in it. To a large degree, their futures will be shaped by their expectations: expecting joy, they will find it; expecting beauty, they will recognize it; and expecting love, they will experience it.

Because the child from two to three years old is learning so many new things, parents are faced with an awesome responsibility and a magnificent opportunity. We can help our children feel confident about themselves and their ability to cope with new situations. We can help them discover a wider world by providing a secure home base. Perhaps most important of all, we can provide our children with a reservoir of happy memories. Sometimes the very best thing to do is to turn our backs on the future and focus on the here and now, for with every moment of joy and with every exposure to beauty, we are building their memories.

Chapter 2
EVERYDAY LIVING

After the third story, the fourth good night kiss, and the second glass of water, Karen's mother threw herself down on the living room sofa muttering to her husband, "She's the worst part and the best part of every day of my life." The sentiment that Karen's mother expressed was shared by many of the parents we visited. Whether they described their two-year olds as fantastic or impossible, they always added a "but" or an "except."

> Peter is the most hard-headed kid in the world, but he's so much fun to live with.

> Jessica is the ideal child except when we suggest bedtime.

> Andrea is the most mild-mannered of all my kids, but she's a holy terror at mealtime.

Most of the negative attributes that parents complained about were associated with daily routines. Confrontations occurred as the two-year olds increasingly asserted their autonomy and sought to control decision-making. Billy's mother, for example, related a typical story. While the whole family was standing on one leg waiting to go shopping, Billy insisted on fastening his jacket by himself. Then at bedtime, when asked to pull his shirt off, he demanded that "Mommy do."

Eventually all parents are placed in a position where they must exercise authority. However, this is not necessarily a negative outcome. Conflict situations provide parents with an opportunity to establish sensible rules, to set limits, to teach values and to help children make appropriate decisions. Daily routines also are the source of some of the greatest pleasures in parenting. Many parents reported that shared cleaning-up and fixing-up activities, mealtime conversations, and before-bed-cuddle-time were the "best part" of their day.

From our talks with different families about the kinds of concerns they have regarding routines, we can make two broad generalizations. First, the situations that bring about conflict reflect the value system of the family. Parents who are particularly concerned about nutrition are likely to have conflicts around food. Parents who emphasize the importance of sleep often have trouble over naps and bedtime. Parents who are concerned with teaching independence have more than the usual number of confrontations over self-help skills, such as dressing and toilet training.

Second, each family has a distinctive style for meeting conflict. Despite a bewildering variety of situations, there is a pattern of consistency in the way routine problems are handled. Each family's style is a unique blend of strategies, some aimed at avoiding conflict and others directed toward resolving conflict. We will begin this chapter by discussing these two characteristics of a family's style and spend the remainder of the chapter reviewing the routines that punctuate a day in the life of a two-year old. We will see that there are a variety of ways parents can translate their individual styles into specific problem-solving techniques.

Ways of Avoiding Conflict

Planning Ahead and Setting Rules

Andy was particularly fond of a pair of overalls with two pockets that he had inherited from his older brother. Most of the time his mother was perfectly happy to wash them at night and let him wear them in the morning,

but there were exceptions. Easter morning was one of those exceptions, and Andy's mother was not about to let him go to church in tattered overalls. The night before Easter, with the overalls still in the wash, she suggested to Andy that they go to his closet and choose an outfit for church. Andy took a while to decide between the blue pants and the green pants, but he finally made his decision.

Clearly, it is impossible to plan ahead all the time. On some occasions, two year old children actually become more difficult to live with if they are told what is coming. Anticipating a very exciting experience, they cannot wait; or dreading an upcoming event, they stew about it. In general, though, two-year olds are much more amenable to parental plans when they know about them a few hours, or perhaps a day, in advance.

Planning ahead is facilitated by setting up rules that two-year olds can learn and follow. The daily routine then becomes predictable and children can act accordingly. Children as young as two years old are capable of obeying a rule if it is stated clearly and firmly: "No walking in the road." "No cookies in the morning." Often parents find that this rule setting is even more effective when the rules are stated in a more positive way: "You may go out as far as the sidewalk." "Cookies are for afternoon snack."

Two-year olds usually learn these rules informally as different situations arise. In Heath and Colby's family, the parents reinforced this kind of learning by holding family meetings. Once a month the family gathered in the

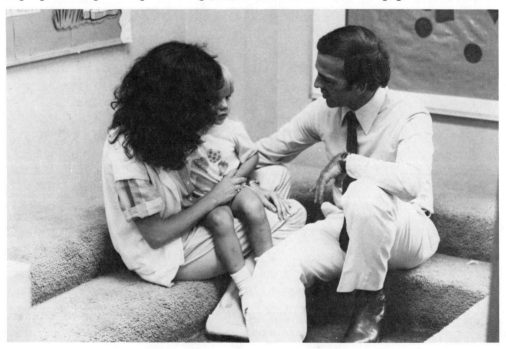

family room, where the twins drank milk from coffee cups and their mother served cinnamon rolls. The parents restated those rules the children were having trouble observing, and the whole family discussed special activities that Heath and Colby were allowed to do, such as mixing the orange juice, getting the newspaper, and operating the garage door opener. Heath and Colby's parents described holidays and other memorable events that would occur soon, and each member of the family was given a job. At Thanksgiving, for example, Heath was the roll man and Colby was the cranberry man. Despite their tender age, Heath and Colby enjoyed these family meetings and listened attentively to the discussion.

Whether rules are presented casually or systematically, it is best to apply them consistently. At the same time, situations are always changing, children are growing, and parents are developing new insights. Yesterday's rule may not be as good as today's idea. We visited one home in which the mother assured us that there were *never* exceptions to rules like, "No dessert unless you finish your meal," or "No playing with things in stores." This degree of consistency seems artificially rigid. It does not help children learn about compromise which may be the rule in many real world settings.

Distraction

Parents can often avoid conflict with very young children by cheerfully removing them from troublesome situations. At other times, children can be given a substitute object to replace one that has been taken from them. As children grow older, however, they hold onto their ideas more tenaciously and it is harder to distract them. Some fast talking and imagination may be needed to make a distraction work. Ryan, for example, was going through a stage of refusing to drink his milk. One evening Ryan's father decided to try distracting him with a pretend game.

> Father: "Oh, I know what's wrong with this milk. It needs a little ketchup in it." (Pretending to pour the ketchup in the milk.) "There – now I'm sure it will taste good. Try it and see."
>
> Ryan: (Grabbing the milk and taking a sip.) "It tastes terrible!"
>
> Father: "It does?" (Sounding incredulous.) "Oh, of course. I know what's missing. Just a sprinkle of meow mix. Now I'm *positive* it will taste good."
>
> Ryan: (Grabbing the milk and trying it again.) "It tastes terrible, terrible!"

Distraction is an excellent way to avoid conflict when the reason for a parental request is complicated and hard to explain. Two year old children have difficulty understanding why they should eat certain foods but not others, why they have to go to bed at a certain hour, or why they cannot take a friend's toy home with them. Using humor and imagination to distract a child in these situations puts off the conflict until a later day, when perhaps the child will be better able to understand an explanation.

In Ryan's case, the distraction worked because it appealed to a two-year old's sense of autonomy. Even though his father was only pretending to doctor the milk, Ryan enjoyed the opportunity to prove him wrong. Distraction also has definite limitations. Both parents and children have to be in the right mood. Parents need to feel fairly relaxed in order to be funny or imaginative, and children must have some flexibility in their position as well. Distraction does not work with a really serious conflict, or when there is not enough time to play games.

No Contest

A final way of avoiding conflict is to develop a very loose schedule in which children participate in the routines of their parents and parents participate in the routines of their children. When we arrived at Mary's house, she was standing at the door with a cold hot dog in her hand. "One for me and one for you," she sang to a bedraggled rag doll as she held the piece of hot dog up to its embroidered mouth. Mary's mother explained casually that the hot dog was Mary's breakfast. Mary always decides what she wants for breakfast and assists in its preparation.

After breakfast, Mary and her mother do the housework together. Because Mary's mother sets a slow pace, Mary is able to join in. Mary plays with toys some of the time, but much of her play consists of helping or imitating her mother. We watched them clean a sliding class door, Mary on one side and her mother on the other. At lunch time Mary set the table, which was another favorite activity. As she put the silverware around the table, her mother capitalized on the teaching opportunity. "Good, you remembered to take out three forks--one for Mommy, one for Daddy, and one for Mary."

This way of avoiding conflict is more than a technique. It is a lifestyle. We were impressed by the tranquility and intimacy that this approach to child rearing seemed to engender. Obviously it is limited to families with a small number of young children. More importantly, it requires a very child-centered world view in which parents can accept the leisurely pace and indifference toward clutter that comes naturally to children. We visited many parents who felt guilty because they did not enjoy spending all day associating with their children. Yet we do not feel that all parents need to be as child-centered as Mary's mother. This approach works well for parents who feel comfortable with it, but it can backfire when parents try to force themselves into such a role. Even the most child-centered parents will sometimes feel constrained adapting their activities to fit into a two-year old's world.

Ways of Resolving Conflict

Explanation

The most common-sense technique for resolving a conflict is to talk about it. Words are very powerful for the two-year old, and parents can often accomplish miracles by offering a serious explanation.

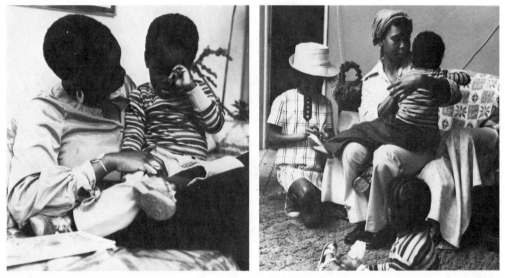

A well-meaning relative had given Kori her first box of lollipops. Although Kori's parents were certain that a well-balanced diet would keep Kori from developing a "sweet tooth," they turned out to be wrong. Kori loved the lollipops and wanted to eat them for dinner. Her father thought this was a good opportunity to teach Kori about nutrition. He had no idea how much she would understand, but he gave Kori a brief explanation about the importance of protein. Kori forgot about the lollipops and went into the bedroom to get Raggedy Ann.

"Want your dinner, Raggedy? What you want for dinner? No lollipops. No, no lollipops. You want yogurt? Yogurt has protein. Special K has protein."

Naturally, explanations do not work all the time. Sometimes a two-year old isn't verbal enough to follow an explanation. Other times the child uses the "Let's talk about it" technique as manipulation. Brenan had gone to bed past his bedtime and was in that state parents always dread, where he was simply too tired to go to sleep. After bringing two snacks and telling several bald-headed chicken stories, his father finally said, "Now it's really time to go to sleep – good night and no more calling." As soon as his father had left the room, Brenan began to cry bitterly. This time his mother went into the room. "Okay, Brenan, stop crying," she stated firmly. "Let's talk about it." Brenan countered, "Let's talk about it in the living room."

Explaining rules to children actually encourages them to respond verbally. The children try to match their parents' reasons with reasons of their own. Although their arguments may be crude and far from logical, parents who genuinely believe in explaining things to children will find themselves compromising. Some of the time the children will have a point.

Rewards and Punishments

When a two-year old refuses to accept an explanation and a compromise solution is not possible, parents are placed in a position of invoking a stronger

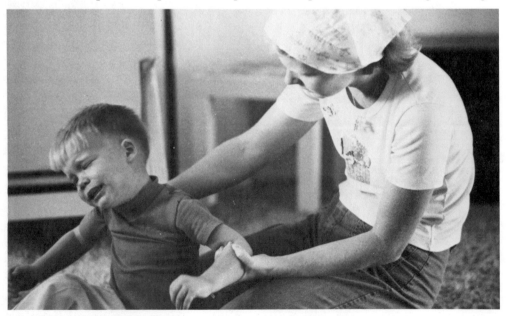

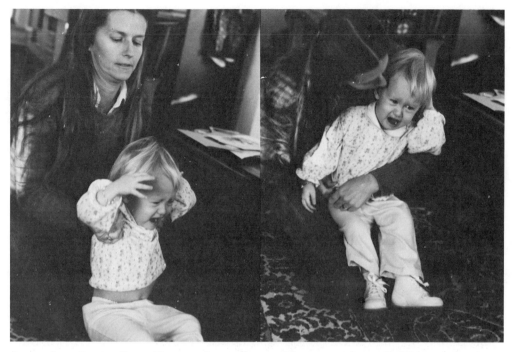

form of authority. Broadly speaking, they can try to induce children to go along with them by offering some kind of reward, or they can coerce the children by using some form of punishment.

The parents with whom we talked used rewards extensively. In fact, all the techniques for avoiding conflict can be described as rewards. Children feel rewarded when they are included in future plans, offered a pleasant distraction, praised for following a rule, or allowed to share a common activity with parents. Rewards were also used on a systematic basis to overcome outstanding problems such as using the toilet, shopping in the grocery store, and taking medicine. However, when resolving the day-to-day conflicts that occur in every family, parents were more likely to use rewards as a last resort than as a preliminary step.

One explanation for this is that it is not always easy to think of an appropriate reward on the spur of the moment. Although most two-year olds respond favorably to candy, many parents are against the idea of using food as a reward. Another reason may be that two-year olds have difficulty understanding the conditionality of a reward. Lennie was told by his parents that, if he was a good boy and let the doctor see his tongue, Daddy would buy him a little car. Lennie was terrified in the doctor's office and had a full-blown temper tantrum. After the visit the real battle began. "I want car." "No," said Daddy, "you cried in the doctor's office." "Car, want car," screamed Lennie, who felt that the very act of seeing the doctor justified the reward.

The primary reason for not using rewards regularly seems to be that parents simply do not think in terms of rewards during a conflict situation. The child's behavior upsets them and they think in terms of punishment. To offer a reward goes against the grain. It is only after a problem recurs frequently, and is of special concern, that parents think through a systematic approach involving some kind of reward.

The kind of punishment mentioned most often by parents was criticism. Typically, they would criticize their child by saying, "I don't like that," or "I'm very mad at you." This kind of statement felt right to the parents. It was emotionally honest. It also was a kind of explanation in that it went beyond saying "Stop it," or "No." The parents were trying to explain how they felt. For the most part, the children seemed to perceive this criticism as a mild punishment. The parents regained their good humor after getting angry feelings off their chest and the children went back to their activities, not much worse for the experience.

Another form of mild punishment was to deprive children of some privilege. The parents reported that denying two-year olds bedtime stories or favorite television programs just because they had been "bad" did not have much impact on the children. However, when the deprivation was logically connected to the misbehavior, the results were somewhat better. For example, when two-year olds wandered away from the yard, and subsequently were not allowed to play outside for a while, the punishment seemed to help them learn the rules.

Logical discipline, however, sometimes goes against common sense. The logical consequence of not taking a nap was being overly tired, but few parents were willing to let their children get in such a state. A logical punishment for being destructive or excessively restless was to restrict the playing space of the child, but several parents found that this approach made their children even more destructive and restless.

For the worst offenses, parents used stronger forms of punishment, such as spanking. Virtually all of them spanked their two-year olds, but there were enormous differences in the amount of spanking, the reasons for spanking, and parents' feelings about spanking. Some children were spanked as infrequently as once or twice a year, while others were spanked several times a day. Even the concept of what constituted a spanking varied for different families. One parent tapped her child lightly on the rear after he ran out in the road, but still felt embarrassed at having used physical punishment. A second parent, who smacked her child on the legs many times during our visit, insisted that she seldom gave her child a spanking. When we questioned her further, we discovered that her definition of spanking was placing the child over her knee and hitting him with a brush.

Despite these differences, the parents seemed to agree that spanking was reasonable in two situations. The first was one in which a child was doing something dangerous, such as playing with an electrical socket or riding a tricycle in the street. The second was when a child was exceptionally aggressive. Children who deliberately hit their parents in the face or bit their parents were very likely to be punished physically.

Even though parents used physical punishment, few of them defended it with much enthusiasm. They realized that spanking often occurred because they had lost control. They also realized that spanking worked because it intimidated the children, and most parents did not really want to foster a feeling of fear in their children.

In talking with the parents it seemed clear to us that there was a residue of guilt over spanking. As long as the parents felt they were not exceeding the "norm" for spanking, and as long as they could justify the spanking as being effective, this guilt did not surface. But when parents found themselves spanking more and more while becoming increasingly less effective, they began to feel frustrated and guilty. "Jeffrey likes to pull the leaves off houseplants," his mother told us. "I have smacked him and smacked him, but the more I spank him, the worse he gets."

A number of parents also told us that they had reconsidered their use of physical punishment when the children started to call their attention to it. When a two-year old suddenly says, "Mommy, don't hit me," it may cause parents to see spanking in a new light.

The other form of strong punishment that parents used was isolation. This technique was the most popular way to handle temper outbursts. Children were told to go to their room (or bed) until they could behave more acceptably. In Brian's family, his father had actually built a fort in the family room. When Brian was defiant, he was sent to his fort to play until all the bad feelings had gone away. Typically, children were allowed to decide when to come out. When they rejoined the family, they were hugged and reassured. Parents were amazed at the transformation in their children, from being defiant to being happy and wanting to please.

At dinner one night, Marty expressed his own exhaustion by making the family miserable. He refused to eat his meat, kicked his sister, and finger painted on the table with his milk. His father issued a firm order. "Go into your room and don't come out until you can eat your dinner." Marty returned in good spirits a few minutes later. After dinner, Marty was on his best behavior and even picked up this toys without being asked. Finally, it was getting late and his mother suggested that they get ready for bed. Marty responded with genuine surprise. "I a good boy. I don't got to go in my room." Following this event, the family selected a back room rather than the bedroom as a cooling-off place.

A similar situation occurred in another family we visited. Antonia's par-

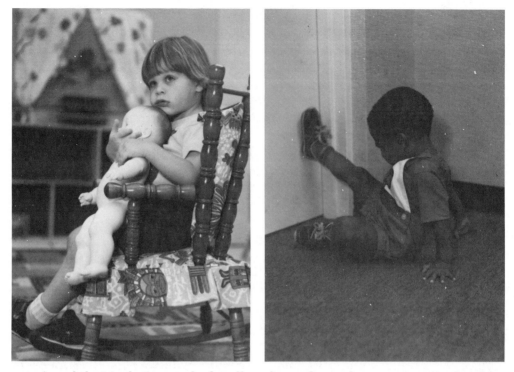

ents found that isolation worked well and sent her to her room routinely when she was out of control. Although daytime behavior improved dramatically, Antonia refused to stay in her room at night. She inevitably crept out of bed and, as the family expressed it, "camped out in the hall." Recognizing that daytime isolation in the bedroom was producing nighttime separation fears, the family placed a "time-out" chair in the kitchen and the nighttime fears became less intense.

Although many professional psychologists recommend ignoring a temper tantrum, the parents we saw did not respond in this way. They reacted to a temper tantrum by sending the child away. Pretending not to hear a screaming fit was either too difficult or too unnatural. Instead, the parents made it clear that they heard and they disapproved. At the same time they gave the children a way to save face; or perhaps we should say, a way to change face. As soon as they felt better, the children were free to leave their exile and rejoin society.

As we looked at the different techniques that parents used to resolve a conflict, we found ourselves making value judgments. We were concerned about families in which punishment was breaking down the bond of attachment between parents and children. Any form of punishment can become so punitive that it threatens a child with loss of love. This happens when parents use punishment too often. Whether it is spanking, yelling, isolating, or depriving a child of privileges, a punishment loses its power if it is over-used. The children stop responding to their parents because they feel they have little to lose. Both children and parents are caught in a vicious cycle. Parents step up the punishment because it is ineffective, and childen withdraw their allegiance even more. When parents find themselves in this kind of situation, it is time to reduce the level of punishment and concentrate on avoiding conflicts or resolving them through rewards.

Coping With Sticky Problems

Sleeptime

Bedtime problems topped the list of parent concerns among the families we visited. For many families, the problem was getting the child into bed in the first place. The resistance of the children seemed to stem from several different factors. First, they had become aware that bedtime, like other routines, was a decision made by parents. If parents could decide it was time for bed, two-year olds felt they could decide it was not time. In support of their view, two-year olds could point to the fact that other members of the family did not go to bed at the same time as they did. A second reason was that the two-year olds found it increasingly difficult to go to bed and relax

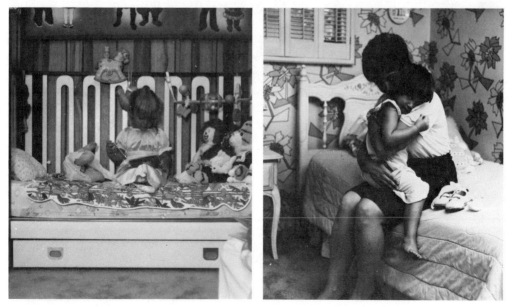

at the end of the day. No longer was it easy for them to forget their memories of the immediate past or their plans for the immediate future. They wanted to hold onto the pleasures of the day, to keep playing just a little longer. Finally, the two-year olds had a new appreciation of their aloneness during sleep. Why should they have to sleep by themselves while their parents got to share a bed? Imaginary fears assailed them in the solitude of their own bedroom.

Most of the children had established bedtime routines at an earlier age. They had learned to get ready for bed by taking a bath or reading a story. They had developed favorite sleeping positions and a variety of comforting behaviors, such as sucking a thumb or stroking a blanket. But these routines proved inadequate as they got older, and going to bed became a recurring battle.

Some parents tried letting the children cry themselves to sleep. While this technique had worked well when the children were less than a year old, the parents found it was far less successful with two-year olds. At this age the children could keep in mind why they were upset and what they wanted to do about it. They could use words as well as screams to communicate their dissatisfaction, and frequently they could get out of their crib or bed if they

wanted to. This is not to say that the technique never worked. Used occasionally, and as a last resort, parents were able to force two-year olds to go to sleep by ignoring them. However, very few of the parents reported that this approach resolved bedtime problems on a regular basis.

Other families went to the opposite extreme and avoided bedtime problems by eliminating any differences between two-year olds and other family members. When it was time for the two-year old to go to bed, all the lights in the house were turned out and everyone went to sleep, usually in the same room. Or alternatively, two-year olds stayed up as long as they wished. If they felt tired, they might lie down and go to sleep in the living room, right in the middle of the family circle. If they did not feel tired, they went to sleep later, when their parents went to bed.

Most of the parents we interviewed took a more moderate approach. They tried to avoid bedtime problems, but without giving up the distinction between grownups and young children. At the same time, they did not use their adult authority to coerce the children into compliance. The parents' general strategy was to make bedtime more attractive for a two-year old. Some families bought a bed to replace the crib; others purchased new sheets with designs that appealed to their children. Some families took advantage of their two-year old's burgeoning imagination and bought new stuffed animals and doll friends for bedtime. However, the essence of this middle-of-the-road approach was to elaborate on the bedtime ritual that had been started earlier. Parents who had read a goodnight story to their children found themselves reading three or four stories. Those who had settled their children with a song found their songs kept getting longer and longer.

Extending and elaborating on the bedtime routine represented a compromise. On the one hand, it communicated to the children that parents understood their feelings about going to bed so prematurely. On the other hand, it communicated to them that parents still had the right to decide when two-year olds ought to go to bed. In effect the bedtime routine served as a reward for two-year olds who accepted parental decision-making.

Sometimes these elaborated bedtime routines became quite unique. For example, in Andy's family the routine was a symbolic game of "Hide and Seek." First, Andy hid in his parent's bedroom and they found him; then the parents hid in Andy's bedroom and he found them. Robert's parents held him up to the bedroom window so that he could say goodnight to all the children in the neighborhood. Then he was put in his crib, whereupon he threw out all the stuffed animals except the monkey. Jodi's mother would hug Jodi, pull away, then come back for another hug and kiss. After three or four of these return hugs, she would leave the room.

Such bedtime routines were not preplanned by the parents but grew spontaneously as different ideas were tried out. Eventually a routine was established that satisfied both parents and children. The parents in the family felt that their particular routine was a reasonable investment of time and did not overly indulge a two year old child. For the two-year olds, the elaborated routine gave them greater control over the process of going to bed, provided a pleasurable last event for the day, and minimized their separation fears. Of course, bedtime was still subject to some hassles because the goals of parents and children diverged. Both enjoyed the intimate interaction, but parents wanted to move toward briefer bedtime routines, while children wanted to draw out this period of special attention.

The pressures that led to elaborate bedtime routines were less evident in families where a two-year old had older siblings. If the two-year old slept in the same room with an older sibling, separation fears were greatly lessened. The two-year old also did not feel singled out when it was time for bed and, therefore, was not as likely to conclude that bedtime was a cruel and unusual punishment. In fact, siblings who slept in the same room often looked forward to a private period of playing and talking before they went to sleep. The parent-child routines that evolved in other families were replaced by child-child routines.

The parents we visited told us that it was not unusual for their two-year olds to wake up in the middle of the night. Many of the children seemed to be experiencing vivid dreams. They talked, yelled, and even cried as they slept; and if a dream awakened them, they often had trouble going back to sleep. If they woke up for some other reason, the darkness and strangeness of the night, as well as their sense of being alone, also seemed to frighten them. Some of the two-year olds took action to solve this kind of problem by themselves. They got up, wandered through the house, and went back to sleep in a more secure spot, usually in their parents' bedroom. There were parents who encouraged this response by providing alternative sleeping places in their bedroom for the children. Other parents roused themselves and took the children back to their own beds.

Once back in the two-year old's bedroom, parents needed to find ways to help the children relax. They called attention to reassuring fixtures in the room: the nightlight, the familiar blanket, the favorite stuffed animal. A mini-routine was developed, such as giving the two-year old a drink of water or juice. Some parents reported that magical rituals calmed their children. Mandy's father, for example, always put a magic kiss on Mandy's forehead to chase away bad dreams. Allison's mother got rid of nighttime monsters by opening the window and pretending to throw them out. But by far the most common and most effective thing parents did was to stay in the child's bedroom until the two-year old fell asleep or was clearly relaxed. Nothing equaled the reassuring presence of parents. Some parents patted their children, some

rocked their children, some lay down on the floor and took a nap.

Like bedtime routines, these various tactics for responding to middle-of-the-night waking were habit forming. Whatever parents started, children expected in the future. A brief routine, such as giving the child a drink or a magical kiss, was easy to maintain because it did not alter basic sleeping arrangements. Letting a two-year old crawl into the parents' bed, or lying down on the child's bed until the child fell asleep, did change basic sleeping arrangements and was harder to keep up night after night. In considering how to respond to middle-of-the-night wakefulness, parents faced a dilemma. The most effective techniques were also the most likely to disrupt their own sleeping pattern.

A few of the two-year olds we observed had severe sleeping problems. They could not go to sleep for hours after going to bed, or awoke screaming in terror on a regular basis. This situation is extremely tiring for both parents and children. When children are having this much difficulty, we recommend that parents make an extra effort to develop a relaxing bedtime routine. The parents may want to arrange for their children to sleep in the same room with them, or they may choose to spend a lot of time in the child's bedroom. In general, we would advise the parents to avoid starting a routine that involves extensive physical contact between parent and child. Reading a book, giving a personality to a stuffed animal, singing a song, or just staying in proximity to the child are preferable techniques because they lead more directly toward the goal of being able to sleep alone. Of course, in the event these techniques do not calm a child, physical reassurances may be needed.

Severe sleeping problems in a two-year old often indicate that the child has a very strong fear of being left alone. This fear is latent in most children and, when it comes to the surface, it takes time to overcome. The strain on parents can become overwhelming, and parents in this situation should not hesitate to seek assistance from pediatricians and psychologists.

Before leaving the subject of sleeptime, let us consider the issue of naps. Between the ages of one and three, the amount of sleep children require gradually decreases. This change in sleep requirements means that many two-year olds are in a transition phase regarding naps. If they take an afternoon nap, they are not ready to go to sleep at their usual bedtime. If they do not take a nap, however, they are cranky and hard to live with during the latter part of the day. Some two-year olds are also cranky after taking a nap, presumably because they sleep so deeply that they cannot wake up easily after an hour or two.

In this sense, naptime is a no-win situation for parents of two-year olds. Either they cope with a fussy child during the dinner hour or they cope with a child who wants to stay up later and later. This choice is a matter for each family to decide. However, based on the experience of the parents we visited, one thing is virtually certain. It will become increasingly more difficult to persuade a two-year old to go to sleep at naptime. All the factors that exist at bedtime also apply to naptime; and in addition, the child is frequently not very tired.

Parents described a number of ingenious naptime routines. Michael's mother found that Michael was willing to take a nap if he was allowed to sleep in his parents' bed. Theresa's mother used a pretend solution to help Theresa nap. "I know that you're not tired, but the dolls are, so please rest with the dolls." The most frequent idea was to substitute a quiet time for naptime. In effect the children were given a choice about napping. They were expected to stay in their rooms and to rest in their beds, but they were allowed to look at books and play with small toys. If they wished to sleep, they could.

This approach reduces the intensity of power struggles over naptime, while at the same time giving parents a break from their two-year olds. Many parents told us that naptime was as important for them as for their children. By retaining the framework of naptime, parents also gain a degree of flexibility. They can urge their children to go to sleep on days when the children seem especially tired, but on other days they can be more casual.

Despite the sleep problems that occur with two year old children, parents need to remind themselves that sleeping is a natural activity. They may try to regulate the sleeping habits of their children for reasons of convenience and health, but some variation is inevitable. There will be ups and downs in the sleeping habits of two-year olds, periods of sleeplessness and periods of steady sleep. Many unusual situations will modify sleeping behavior, such as vacations and holidays, babysitters, illness, even the change to and from Daylight Savings Time. Parents cannot control all these factors; they can never perfect an infallible sleep routine.

The most realistic course is for parents to keep adapting their techniques to new circumstances. It is far easier to make adaptations when both parents take part in resolving sleep problems. Sharing the responsibility for getting a two-year old to sleep, or for reassuring a two-year old in the middle of the night, leaves both Mom and Dad free to enjoy the positive side of sleep routines, for even when all the problems of sleep have been cataloged, it remains true that nothing quite matches a happy goodnight from a child. Receiving a goodnight kiss from a two-year old and seeing the child drift peacefully to sleep is a most rewarding experience for parents.

Mealtime

Some of the happiest moments within each family are associated with eating. These include shared cooking time, birthday parties, picnics, or dinner at a fast food restaurant. On the other hand, some of the most stressful moments in a family are also associated with eating. Although no two families are alike, we found a consistent pattern in the eating problems that were reported. Parents told us repeatedly that breakfast and lunch usually went fine, but the trouble occurred at dinner. Heather's mother related a typical story:

Heather: "I want pasgetti and meatballs. I don't want chicken."

Mother: "Heather, I didn't make any spaghetti, and you love chicken."

Heather: "I want pasgetti and meatballs. I don't like chicken."

Mother: "Heather, you had spaghetti and meatballs for lunch. Here's your chicken."

Heather: "I don't want chicken."

Mother: "I'll give you one last chance. Either you eat your chicken right this minute or I'll take your plate away." (Heather proceeded to play with the chicken; her mother took the food away and the episode ended with a temper tantrum.)

At breakfast and lunch, different members of the family eat different cereals or sandwiches, and two-year olds are often allowed to choose what they want to eat. At dinnertime, the children are expected to eat the meal that has been prepared for the whole family. Two-year olds still know, however, that there is other food in the kitchen which may not be visible and gradually they become bold enough to demand it. Heather realized that there was a can of spaghetti and meatballs in the cupboard, and in her mind it must have seemed unfair that this food could only be opened at lunch.

Dinner is different in other ways, too. For most families it is the most formal meal of the day. The meal lasts longer and children are expected to stay at the table. Brian's father had just come back from a two-day trip. His mother had planned a particularly nice dinner and had even made it a festive occasion by placing candles on the table. Brian sat politely at the table for the first half of the meal, but when his sister asked for more beans and his father said something to his mother that he couldn't understand, Brian grew restless and slipped down from his youth chair. "Brian, please stay at the table," his mother requested. "We want tonight to be a very happy time for all of us." Brian, who saw no connection between happiness and sitting at the

table, shouted "no" defiantly, and dashed around the room. "Brian," his mother cajoled, "I have a lovely dessert for you. As soon as you finish eating your meat, you can have dessert." "I don't want my meat, I want dessert," Brian shouted back. "Brian," his father insisted in a firm voice, "you heard what your mother said. Now let me put you back in your chair."

Staying in his chair is not much of an issue for Brian at breakfast and lunch. He usually watches "Sesame Street" while eating breakfast and he likes to eat lunch on the run. Although he is not supposed to take food into the living room, he can eat a sandwich while playing in the family room or outside on the patio. Breakfast and lunch end when he is through eating. Brian is not required to sit and wait for his sister or parents to finish. The atmosphere is casual and spontaneous. Sometimes the family eats together and other times everyone eats independently.

The formality of dinnertime also means that more emphasis is placed on good manners. Many two-year olds enjoy playing with their food. Chocolate pudding, they discover, makes fine fingerpaint; bread is good for making balls; and peas and lima beans are fun to squash. A limited amount of this play may be tolerated at breakfast or lunch, but at dinnertime parents expect children to use a fork instead of their fingers, to take moderate bites instead of stuffing their mouths with food, and to ask for food instead of grabbing it.

Finally, dinnertime differs in the amount of exclusive attention children receive. Many fathers do not eat breakfast or lunch with the family, so the children are able to enjoy the undivided attention of their mothers during these meals.

> Mother: "What would you like for lunch, Kori? Would you like a peanut butter sandwich or a cheese sandwich?"
>
> Kori: "Cheese sandwich. Make a cheese sandwich."
>
> Mother: "Let's open the refrigerator door. Cheese, where are you hiding? Are you underneath the pickles? No. Are you behind the horseradish?"
>
> Kori: "I'll find the cheese. I'll make the sandwich."
>
> Mother: "Will you make me a sandwich, too? I'm hungry." (Mother and Kori jointly get the sandwiches together and sit at the table.)
>
> Mother: "Would you like to pour your own milk?" (Kori begins to pour the milk into her glass.)
>
> Kori: "Uh-oh, I spilled it!" (Kori wipes up the milk, eats part of the sandwich, and then takes the cheese out of the second half.)
>
> Kori: "I'm making a snowman."
>
> Mother: "Yes, that does look like a snowman. I see his head and his tummy."

In contrast, dinnertime conversation is more likely to revolve around adult-oriented topics, as the parents share their daily experiences with each other. Parents look forward to relaxing during this conversation, but while they are winding down, the two-year old is often winding up. Left out of the conversation, the two-year old becomes irritable and restless. What begins as a quiet evening can end up with a shouting match and an agreement by the parents that "something has to be done about that kid."

Having pointed out the major reasons why mealtime problems occur most often at dinnertime, what can be done about it? Let us return to the scene with Heather and the unwanted chicken dinner. In her exasperation, Heather's mother chose to punish Heather by removing the food from the table. More often than not, parents later regret this kind of hasty response and let their children eat something else. Parents basically do not want to punish children by depriving them of food. Another common first response is to promise the balking two-year old a reward for eating dinner. Typically, the reward is dessert. Here again, parents, even those who regularly use this kind of reward, are uncomfortable about orienting their children toward sweets.

Every family at times uses crude rewards and punishments. However, there are other options for coping with dinnertime problems. These options usually take extra parental energy and ingenuity. Sometimes they take longer to have an effect, and often their probability of being effective is less than a strong punishment or reward. In short, these other options are available when parents are willing to exert themselves and when they are not adamantly committed to winning a battle over food.

Heather's parents could have tried distraction. They might have directed Heather's attention to the other parts of the meal: the salad, the vegetable, or the bread; and then hoped that later in the meal Heather would return to the chicken. Or, if they preferred to tackle the issue of the chicken right away, they might have tried conversational distraction. For example, Heather's mother could have talked about how chicken is called "finger-lickin" because you get to lick it off your fingers.

A magical game might have distracted Heather. What if Heather's father had used the pepper grinder to put a little magical pepper on his own chicken, and then shown Heather how it made the chicken fly through the air and right into his mouth? Would Heather have wanted to use the pepper to make her own piece of chicken fly? Using distraction in this situation might have led to a happier outcome, provided that Heather's parents did not resent the extra effort involved and were willing to let Heather skip the chicken in the event their conversation and games did not change her mind.

Planning ahead represents another option. (Of course, one has to think of this option before a conflict materializes.) Jennifer's mother often took advantage of her daughter's interest in the kitchen by involving her in the preparation of the evening meal: "We have to fix the salad, and shell the peas, and warm the rolls, and set the table. I'm lucky you are here to help me." As Jennifer and her mother shelled the peas, the conversation continued: "I hope everybody sits at the table tonight and finishes dinner. You and I are working so hard to make this dinner nice." "I'm working hard making dinner," Jennifer agreed. Perhaps Heather, like Jennifer, would have liked the dinner better if she had participated in the cooking.

Even when it is too late to involve a child in the cooking of a meal, two-year olds can sometimes be invited to serve themselves. In this way they get to plan, in a limited fashion, what goes on their plate. Chicken is an ideal food for this technique: "Do you want a bone or no bone?" "Do you want a big bone or a little bone?" "Do you want a leg like Mommy, or a wing like Daddy?"

Explanations and a statement of dinnertime rules also might have helped Heather accept the chicken, although such an approach, like distraction or planning ahead, hardly guarantees that a problem will be resolved. Before Heather became too upset, her father might have said something like, "At dinner, Heather, we all eat the same thing because it takes a lot of work for

Mommy to fix dinner." Other rules, of course, are also possible. The rule at Heather's house might be that she tries at least one bite of every food at dinner, and then she can eat something else. Alternatively, the rule might be that Heather is not required to eat any particular food at dinner, but when the meal is over no more food is served until breakfast. Whatever the rule, it is likely to be complicated for a two-year old. But if parents state their rule in a variety of ways over a period of time, it gradually will make an impact on the behavior of the child.

Some families react to dinnertime problems by adopting the strategy we called "no contest." They go to special lengths to avoid facing situations like Heather and the chicken tantrum. One method is to serve a separate dinner to the children. Usually the two-year old and siblings eat before their father comes home from work, and then go to bed soon afterwards. Later, the parents eat by themselves. This approach eliminates many dinnertime conflicts, but in the process it also eliminates most of the daily interaction between the children and their father. A second option is to provide as much freedom at dinner as at lunch and breakfast. There are fewer arguments about food at dinner because the children get to choose, more or less, what is served to them.

Both of these options place a double load on whoever prepares the meals, which is almost always the mother. In many families, where this burden is considered unacceptable, parents try a modified version of "no contest" by relaxing their dinnertime expectations. They encourage, but do not insist on, two-year olds staying in their chairs during dinner. They discourage, but do not punish, poor table manners. During the early part of the meal, when they hope to get the children interested in eating, the parents direct their conversation toward the children. Dessert and coffee time is reserved for grown-up talk.

Each family develops its own techniques for handling mealtime routines. Naturally, no combination works all the time but if parents feel their own mealtime routines need to be re-evaluated, a logical first step is to compare their expectations at dinner with their expectations at other meals. As we have implied throughout this discussion, it is not necessary for expectations to always be the same. However, if expectations become greater at dinner-time, and the rules become stricter, two year old children will need extra time to realize and accept this fact. Parents can help them by approaching dinnertime problems with a broad repertoire of options.

Snacks

Even when families are comfortable with the compromises they have worked out around mealtimes, there still may be a problem with snacks. Families find themselves having to make all kinds of decisions about snacking. How often should my two-year old be allowed to snack? What should the child be allowed to eat? Where should snacking be permitted? But before a family decides what kind of snacking rules to enforce, they have to come to grips with the purpose they want snacking to serve.

The parents we visited gave snacks to children for two major reasons. First, they were allowed because the children seemed to be hungry. Most two-year olds have a relatively small capacity for food. They can feel perfectly full at the end of breakfast and then quite hungry two hours later. The second reason for giving snacks was quite different. Snacks were used as a reward to manage the behavior of children. Although families differed a great deal in their use of food as a reward, almost all families used it to some extent.

When snacks were used to tide children over between meals, nutritional foods were emphasized, and children were surprisingly receptive to them:

"My tummy needs a snack," Angela insisted as she pulled her mother into the kitchen.

"Well, I guess it does," her mother responded. "Do you suppose your tummy would like celery with cottage cheese in it, or a box of raisins?"

"I suppose wants raisins, " Angela decided. (At this point Angela brought out a snack tray.) "How about I eat my snack on the porch?"

"Fine idea," her mother agreed.

Even the child who refuses vegetables at meal time may be delighted with a snack that consists of a piece of fruit, a strip of raw carrot, a slice of cucumber, uncooked squash, or cauliflower. Other nutritious snacks that families used included squares of cheese, frozen yogurt, sunflower seeds, peanut butter on celery, and frozen fruit juice.

When using food as a reward, parents were much more likely to resort to sweets or junk food. Common examples included giving children candy for learning to use the toilet, putting medicine in a sweetened drink, and distributing cookies to stop their crying.

By using snacks in these two different ways, the parents sent contradictory messages to their two-year olds. One message was that eating nutritious foods is important. The other message was that eating sweets is a sign of good behavior. On the one hand parents were discouraging sweets as not nutritious, but on the other hand they were increasing the significance of these sweets by linking them to good behavior.

This inconsistency came about for a good reason. The parents sincerely wanted their children to eat nutritious foods, but at the same time they did not want to give up the very effective technique of offering sweets as a means of managing behavior. Parents in this situation need to recognize their inconsistency and anticipate a similar kind of ambivalence in their children. The children may accept the importance of eating nutritious food but still have a strong desire for sweets and junk food.

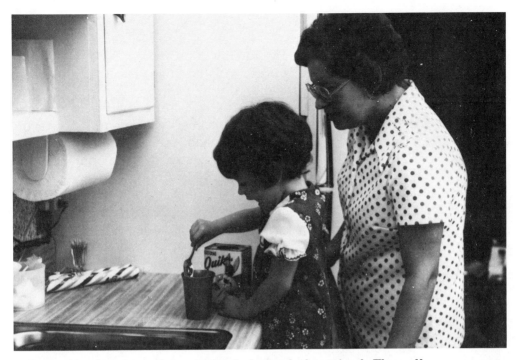

Some families try to be completely logical about food. They allow no sweets or junk food in the house. However, it usually turns out that their children discover nutritious substitutes which are heavily sweetened, such as yogurt or cereal. We also found that when a certain sweet or junk food is completely prohibited, it turns into a "forbidden fruit" and is craved all the more. Parents who are concerned about limiting non-nutritious foods seem to have greater success when they adopt a less dogmatic position. The parents do not keep sweets or junk food around the house, but they also do not get upset if their children occasionally eat such food as a treat.

From a two-year old's point of view, snacks provide an important means of expressing autonomy. Like Angela, many children are given an opportunity to make a limited choice. They are permitted to feed themselves snack food and, within limits, to choose where to eat it. Angela even enjoyed following her mother's rule about using a snack tray because she perceived it as an opportunity to be grown up.

Where families allow children to take part in making a snack, there are extra bonuses. The children not only develop fine motor skills by spreading, mixing, pouring, and spooning, they also learn to use language to describe their various activities. Whether separating the sections of a tangerine, dipping a butter spreader into a jar of peanut butter, or watching frozen yogurt melt in the heat, the children are learning about "science" through a hands-on approach.

Toilet Training

Toilet training is a major issue for parents of two-year olds. While it may not make much difference to the children whether they learn to use the toilet at twenty-four or thirty-six months of age, this twelve month span usually makes a big difference to parents. The messy diaper that was changed cheerfully during toddlerhood begins to produce frustration and rage as the child gets older. Parents do not want to force toilet training on their two-year olds, but their expectations lead them to apply some degree of pressure.

The parents we visited who approached toilet training with moderate expectations handled this dilemma most easily. They actively urged their children to develop self-control, without worrying that toilet training was fraught with symbolic significance. They did not assume that a few mistakes on their part would result in deep psychological trauma to a two-year old. At the same time these parents did not believe that toilet training was as simple and mundane a matter as some psychologists claim. They anticipated that it would take a number of months, rather than a few days, to shape the child's behavior. In short, the parents with moderate expectations adopted a common sense philosophy. Toilet training was seen as a substantial but ordinary challenge for two-year olds.

Most of the parents we talked with were convinced that toilet training should be delayed until their children had sufficient neuromuscular coordination to control bowel and bladder functions. However, since it was not always easy to tell when this point of maturation had been reached, the parents were a bit unsure about when to begin. Many of the parents had started toilet training, at least on a casual basis, between eighteen and twenty-four months.

They invited the children into the bathroom as often as possible, showed them what was happening, and let them help flush the toilet. They encouraged the childen to sit on the toilet themselves and in this way discovered if the child preferred a regular toilet, a portable toilet, or a potty chair that fit on the regular toilet.

By the age of two, many children will respond to this kind of consistent but low-key approach. Even if they are only interested in placing a doll on the toilet or flushing the toilet, it is a beginning. The next step is to help the children have some successful experiences while sitting on the toilet and to demonstrate to them that they can do what is expected. Ideally, this step should not be initiated until it is clear that a child enjoys sitting on the toilet and feels relaxed. The more relaxed the child feels, the longer that child will stay seated on the toilet, and the greater the likelihood that urination or elimi-nation will occur. Parents need to feel relaxed as well, for their mood will be picked up by the children.

Grandparents, friends, and "experts" on toilet training may be able to suggest some gimmicks for getting things started. For example, the faucet in the bathroom sink can be turned on and the child's attention directed to it. The sight and sound of running water causes some children to sympa-thetically urinate. Before taking a bath, a child can step into a tub of warm water, then get back out and go to the bathroom. The warm water induces urination, and many children first observe their ability to urinate when in the bathtub. Or a child can drink something while sitting on the toilet. Again, drinking stimulates urination.

When parents and children start this phase of toilet training, they will be watching closely for any sign of success. The sight of a urine stream de-scending into the toilet will be an exciting moment, the feeling of accom-plishment will be keen. (Some parents sit their children backwards on the toilet so that it is easier for them to see the urine go into the toilet.) As ex-cited as parents and children get when these success experiences occur, the truth is that, in the beginning, failures (or non-successes) take place much more frequently. Parents need to keep this fact in mind when responding to a child's first success. It is natural to exclaim enthusiastically, "Oh, you're really a big boy (or girl) now." But what about all the times in the beginning when nothing happens, or when the children have accidents? In these sit-uations the parents do not want their children to feel they have lost the sta-tus of big boys and girls. In the first stages it is helpful if parents praise their children in concrete terms: "You're really learning how to use the toi-let!" "Look what you did – that's great!" Later, when successes far outnum-ber failures, the global identification of toilet training with growing up is more appropriate.

As a child's success experiences begin to occur with some regularity,

parents may decide to start training in earnest. At this point children can switch from diapers to underpants. Toilet training is difficult to complete when children are left in diapers. The children cannot easily remove the diapers in order to sit on the toilet. Pulling underpants up and down takes some practice, but it paves the way to greater independence. In addition, children may have become accustomed, perhaps even comfortable, going to the bathroom in their diapers. Putting them in underpants breaks this association.

Underpants are a clear symbol to the children that parents now trust them to use the toilet faithfully, for accidents will have much more conspicuous consequences. Some of the parents we visited found that giving a child pretty underpants provided a tremendous boost to toilet training. The children did not want to wet or soil these special clothes. Other children, although they liked the idea of wearing underpants, were not so overwhelmed.

In either event there usually was a period during which accidents occurred with great frequency. Even though the parents were understanding about these accidents, they often felt that they were making no progress. Fortunately, when they look back a year or two later, they probably won't remember these first accidents. And, in reality, most children who have reached the underpants stage in a positive frame of mind are toilet trained during the daytime in a surprisingly short period of time. Staying dry during the night is another matter, and for many children this will not be mastered for several more years.

To be sure, toilet training does not always follow the sequence we have outlined. Sometimes a hitch develops and parents and children get bogged down in a power struggle. Most often the hitch is over bowel training. A bowel movement is harder to produce and therefore requires a higher level of relaxation. It also occurs less frequently. For both these reasons children have less incentive to use the toilet. They find it easier to eliminate in the familiar diaper, and after having been cleaned up, they are through with the problem for the rest of the day. Frequently, children who resist bowel training have selected a private place of their own in which to have a bowel movement:

behind the couch, in a particular corner, in a back room of the house. As parents try to persuade such children to use the toilet instead, these two-year olds become even more insistent on following their own ideas. Their sense of being in control, of making decisions, is now running counter to the goals of toilet training. The parents and the children are on a collision course.

Some of the parents who found themselves in this situation decided to put off toilet training until their children were older. This decision defused the power struggle, but in itself did not guarantee the toilet training would be any easier in the future. Toilet training was already established as an area of conflict in the family, and unless some new factors enter the picture, the conflict is likely to reappear in the future. Of course, new factors are always appearing, and perhaps one of them will change the child's attitude toward toilet training and make the process easier the next time it is tried.

On the other hand, parents in this situation may consciously try to introduce new factors that will dissipate the power struggle between parent and child and allow toilet training to proceed. One approach is to offer more rewards for using the toilet. The greatest reward for a two-year old is the positive attention of parents. Parents can increase the amount of positive attention associated with toilet training by turning a two-year old's trip to the bathroom into a social occasion.

Bathroom time can become a time when parents and children play and

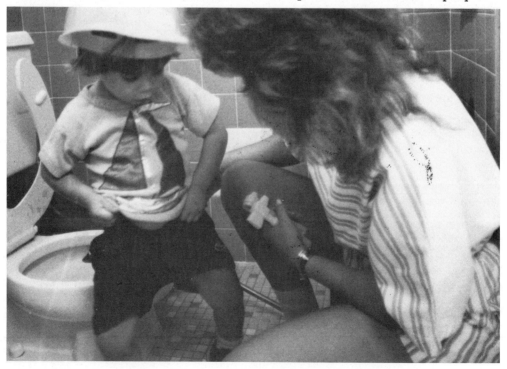

talk together. For example, a parent might read stories to a child while the child sits on the toilet. They might sit together in the bathroom for ten to twenty minutes each day during a time when a bowel movement is probable. Even if nothing happens at first, the confrontation over where to go to the bathroom will be eased as the child associates pleasant experiences with sitting on the toilet. Alternatively, the parent and child might play with little cars and trucks, dolls, or any other toy that interests the child sufficiently to stay on the toilet for a period of time.

Turning bathroom time into parent-child playtime will be somewhat awkward for most parents and children. Play does not flow as smoothly when one party is sitting on a toilet. If the technique works, it also may lead to bathroom rituals in which the children depend on certain playthings whenever they go to the bathroom. This ritualistic behavior may be less functional than a straightforward, no-nonsense use of the toilet, but it is not a serious problem.

Parents who do not wish to start a pattern of playing with their children during bathroom time may introduce new factors in other ways. Some two-year olds are fascinated with the variety of toilets that can be discovered in their environment. (Other two-year olds, of course, are frightened by unfamiliar toilets.) Parents can encourage this kind of two-year old to use toilets in restaurants, stores, the homes of friends, wherever there is a new and different toilet. Again, the child may only sit on the toilet at first, but eventually, if the child remains interested in exploring bathrooms, the toilet will be used.

Another way to break an impasse over toilet training is to enlist the aid of an adult whom the two-year old likes and trusts. Toilet training may temporarily be discontinued at home, but whenever the child visits this particular neighbor or relative, the new adult can encourage the child to use the toilet. In effect, the two-year old gets a fresh start on toilet training with a different authority figure. In this new situation, the child's desire to please may be greater than feelings of resistance toward toilet training.

Still another new factor that parents can introduce is peer pressure. Pressure is not really the right word, for the imitative bathroom behavior of a group of two and three-year olds is more like a game, or a party. Parents can arrange for their two-year old to accompany a friend to the bathroom, to watch, and then to take a turn on the toilet. Young friends enjoy going to the bathroom together, and the desire to be a part of this activity is a powerful motivation for any two-year old. Peer modeling, peer encouragement, and even peer praise represent important resources for the parent who is having trouble toilet training a two-year old.

The same kind of benefits can occur when untrained two-year olds go to a school or child care setting. However, there the peer interaction needs to be monitored more closely by an adult. Because a child arrives as a stranger in a large group of children, a situation can develop in which peers tease and ostracize the untrained child. When children are close to being trained, this problem is not likely to persist. In a short time the children learn to use the toilet and are accepted by the other children. When a child is not close to being trained, however, an adult should be available to ensure that the child is not persecuted. In practice this is relatively easy, for the new child will soon make a friend or two, and the teacher can encourage the child to go to the bathroom with these friends. In addition, the teacher can handle toileting accidents in a matter-of-fact way, explaining to the other children that the untrained child is learning how to use the toilet. On balance, young children are very supportive of each other when it comes to toilet training, and any negative responses are easily managed by an observant adult.

Even after children are basically trained, new challenges sometimes appear. For example, it is not unusual for children between the ages of two and four to try going to the bathroom outside – either because they cannot be bothered making the trip indoors or just because it is fun. This experimentation generally dies down in a few weeks or months, but in some cases the behavior takes a turn for the worse. The children start making a special point of going to the bathroom in inappropriate places, and they may begin to wet and soil themselves out of defiance. Confrontations again boil up between parents and children, and extra effort is required to de-escalate the conflict.

In the event the children continue to express their anger with unacceptable toileting behavior, the parents need to seek the help of a child psychologist. This kind of behavior is not only a counterproductive way for the children to express anger, it also can have serious negative repercussions on relationships within the family.

The whole issue of toilet training is less formidable since the advent of disposable diapers. Still, it is wise for parents of two-year olds to think about their own expectations. Putting off toilet training too long may mean that they lose their patience before the training is completed. At the same time it is important for parents to keep reminding themselves that in good time all children are toilet trained.

Dressing

Terry's mother greeted us at the door. "Just in time," she assured us. "I just got Terry dressed up and ready for his picture." At this moment Terry strolled into the room. On top he was wearing an attractive plaid shirt neatly buttoned up; on the bottom he was wearing nothing. "Oh, no, not again," his mother sounded off in dismay. "Ever since this kid learned to undress himself, I can't get him to keep his clothes on."

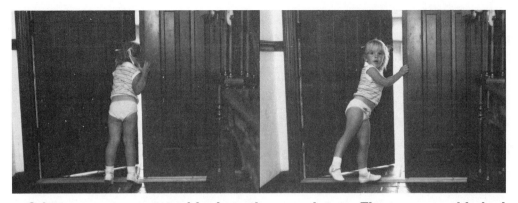

Other parents we visited had similar complaints. The two-year olds had mastered the ability to take their clothes off, and much of the time they preferred to go naked around the house. When it came time to get dressed, they resisted either by running away, or they peeled off their clothes almost as quickly as parents could get them on. This tendency of two-year olds to prefer nudity sometimes led to a power struggle over dressing. The children felt it was their right to remain in a state of undress, while the parents felt just as strongly that it was their responsibility to keep the children dressed.

Some parents seemed to fear that other adults would be shocked by a two-year old's bareness. They worried that others would critically judge them for being negligent parents. At times the parents also voiced a concern that their children would be cold without clothes and would get sick. Beyond these specific objections, however, there seemed to be a general uneasiness about prolonged periods of nudity, a vague notion that if two-year olds did not learn to wear clothes at this age, they might grow up without a sense of modesty.

These parental fears stem from legitimate concerns, but if parents examine them more closely, they may be able to avoid confrontations over dressing. Parental fears about being judged harshly, for example, may be justified in certain public places, but are much less plausible in a home setting. Many people who might raise their eyebrows over a naked two-year old at church would be delighted to see the same child cavorting at home. Parental fears about naked children catching cold also make more sense in some situations than in others. Outside on a cool day, or inside in a particularly drafty room, children may become genuinely chilled and lose some of their resistance to germs. At the same time, their high level of activity seems to keep them from getting chilled long past the point that would bother adults. Parental fears, once they have been admitted, about two-year olds not learning modesty may seem a little silly. At two years of age, children can hardly be expected to understand the complicated idea that the human body is beautiful but nevertheless needs to be covered in certain ways most of the time.

In short, reflecting on parental concerns about nakedness can often lead to compromise. Parents may decide that it is all right to remain undressed at home, but clothes must be worn when going out in public. It may be all right to stay in a warm house without clothes, but not all right to go outside when the weather is cool. It may be acceptable to play naked in a part of the house that is comfortably warm, but in a cold basement or a drafty room one must be dressed. Naturally, these compromises do not eliminate all disagreements and misunderstandings, but they help focus attention on the dressing requirements of specific situations. Struggles over who has the most power are reduced in intensity.

Although many two-year olds revel in nakedness, they also are intrigued by certain clothes. These clothes become important possessions and are a part of their sense of identity. Shoes are the most common example. Some children get attached to one pair of shoes and refuse to wear any others. They act as if changing to different shoes would change them in some sort of disasterous way. Kori, for example, became attached to a pair of red sneakers and insisted on wearing them with a long pink party dress at Thanksgiving dinner. Other children are more like Jon, who decided that his sandals were for playing at the park, his sneakers were for nursery school, and his brown shoes were for McDonald's. Some children refuse to wear any shoes at all, but still insist on carrying favorites around with them.

It is understandable that shoes are promoted to positions of honor and distinction. For one thing, they go on feet; and from the moment babies first discover their own toes, feet hold a special fascination. Furthermore, from a child's point of view, the rituals in the shoestore make the buying of shoes an awesome occasion. The child sits down in a special chair and a strange adult comes over with a big silver shining thing. The silver thing closes it-

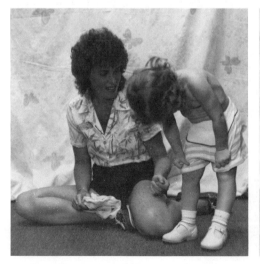

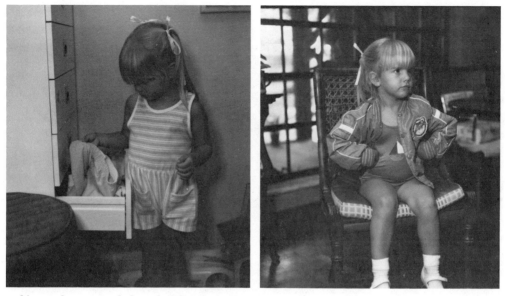

self gently around the child's foot. Then the strange adult brings out an armful of boxes. This stranger keeps taking shoes out of the boxes and fitting them on until just the right shoe is found. Then, with even greater solemnity, the shoes get wrapped up and paid for. The shoes, with their new smell and new feel, are ready to be taken home. Tomorrow, as the shoes run and jump, they will gaily testify to all concerned that the child inside them has indeed grown bigger.

Recognizing that certain clothes have extra meaning for two-year olds, most of the parents we visited did let their children help decide what to wear. Inevitably there were some problems. From a parent's viewpoint, the children seemed excessively rigid. "Why must it be the same dress every Sunday?" thought Jenny's mother. Jenny was attached to a dress that had bells sewn into the hem which she called her ring-ding dress. From a child's viewpoint, however, it may seem that parents are rather rigid in their ideas, too. Parents seem to have the peculiar notion that certain clothes do not go with each other, like red sneakers with a pink party dress.

Even when parents do not insist that their children look stylish, limits have to be set on the free choice of clothing. There are times when children insist upon wearing something that either is or ought to be in the washing machine. There are also hot days when children decide to wear a turtleneck sweater and cold days when they would like to wear shorts. These inappropriate choices can become opportunities for showing children how to compromise.

Jason's grandmother bought him a pair of swimming trunks with a sailboat appliqué. Not surprisingly, Jason wanted to wear his "boat pants" the

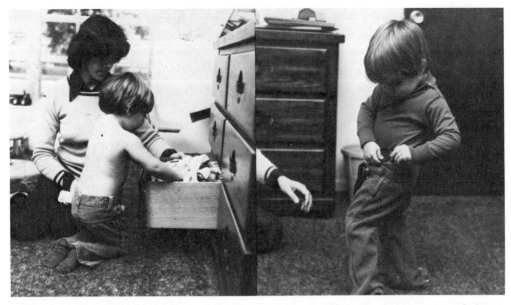

next morning even though it was snowing out. "You can't go out with boat pants," his mother explained. "Boat pants are for summer when it's hot." "I'll tell you what," his mother suggested. "We will put your boat pants on now and pretend it's summer. Then, before you go out, we will put on long pants."

When two-year olds are intent on wearing favorite clothes, they may show considerable interest in learning how to dress themselves. Being able to put on new shoes, or a favorite dress, is a clear demonstration of personal autonomy. Some two-year olds, particularly if they have older siblings, adopt dressing skills as a sign of being grown up. These children will spend long hours practicing. We watched Keisha, for example, struggle patiently for fifteen minutes to buckle a pair of sandals. When she stood up, they were on the wrong feet. No matter, she sat down again and spent another fifteen minutes switching them around.

Two-year olds who are intent on practicing dressing skills may even get in the habit of changing their clothes several times a day. This habit can be distressing to parents because the clothes that are removed are left all over the house, and the dresser where the child's clothes are kept usually looks as if a cyclone had hit it. Frustrating as this behavior is, parents can console themselves with the thought that their child is already learning how to be independent in the important area of dressing.

Many parents find that their two-year olds show little interest in learning how to dress themselves. In these families the parents have often established a pattern in which dressing is a leisurely social occasion. It has been a time when the parents and children converse, play silly games and sing songs. Parents need to recognize that children with this kind of experience are going to learn to dress themselves later than other children. The children resist dressing themselves because they enjoy both the social stimulation and the feeling of being waited upon. Their way of expressing autonomy is to insist that this pattern be continued.

Parents in this kind of situation will be most effective if they try to make learning how to dress a part of a social occasion as well. Pete's mother, for example, suggested that they take turns. "My turn with your socks," she said cheerfully as she put the socks on. "Now it's your turn to pull them up." She always engineered the sharing so that Pete finished the task. Kelly's mother used singing. As Kelly stuck her arms through the sleeves in her shirt, her mother sang, "This is the way Kelly puts on her shirt, puts on her shirt, puts on her shirt." Gradually Kelly assumed more and more responsibility for putting on her clothes until her mother's job was reduced to singing.

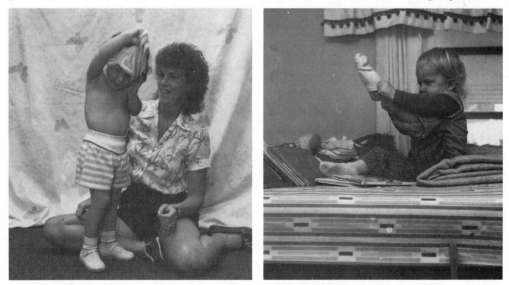

Whether two-year olds are oriented primarily toward dressing or undressing, they make a great deal of progress during this year. There still will be many things about dressing they do not understand or cannot accept, but this should come as no surprise. A family's rules governing the purchase, use, and care of clothing are very complicated. Two-year olds start by focusing on what they can put on or take off their own bodies. Parents will find many opportunities to expand this limited vision, to show children how clothes proceed from the dirty clothes hamper through the washing and drying cycle and to the appropriate dresser; how old clothes wear out and new ones are bought; how clothes become too small, too thin, or too stained. Learning the skills of dressing is just the beginning.

Washing Up

When we arrived at Danielle's house, she was finishing a breakfast of French toast and syrup. "I wash my hands all by myself," she told her father as he helped her down from the high chair. "Cold water first," she told herself as she turned on the right hand faucet. After a good five minutes of hand scrubbing, Danielle's father suggested that her hands were clean and handed her a towel. Like most two-year olds, Danielle enjoyed washing her hands as long as she could play in the water.

Brushing teeth is also a favorite activity for most two-year olds. It is a new accomplishment that allows them to play with water and makes them feel grown-up. Squeezing the toothpaste is a great deal of fun and, if parents do not supervise carefully, a large portion of the tube gets used in a single brushing.

Unless parents mention the nasty term "hair wash," bath time is also great fun for most two-year olds. Any earlier fears of going down the drain have probably been conquered by now, and the children enjoy splashing, pouring, making waves, and mixing the water with soap. A favorite activity is lining up toys on the side of the tub and making them dive in.

Hair washing is quite a different story. Most two-year olds at some time or other have gotten soapy water in their eyes and have become very resistant to hair washing. Laurie, for example, was basically a mild and pliable child who followed her parents' suggestions. But the sight of a shampoo bottle sent her into a frenzy. Hair wash night was dreaded as much by her parents as it was by her, but finally her mother got an idea. She took Laurie to the beauty parlor and let her watch several ladies getting their hair washed. That night Laurie and her mother played beauty parlor. They sat Laurie's doll on the edge of the bathtub, and Laurie became the shampoo lady. "Stay still, and keep your head back, Doll," her mother commented. "Don't cry, Doll," her mother went on, "Laurie won't let the soap get in your eyes." After a while Laurie agreed to put a tiny, tiny bit of shampoo into her own hair, and her mother became the shampoo lady.

Shampooing a doll's hair is an excellent way to desensitize children who are so terrified of hairwashing that they will not let parents put the shampoo in their hair. A related technique is to encourage a two-year old to put shampoo in a parent's hair. Still another idea is to let children watch themselves in a mirror while the shampoo is put on their hair. The white lather that appears gives them an interesting crown, and they may be intrigued by the effect.

Once children have accepted the idea of shampoo in their hair, parents must figure out how they can rinse the shampoo away. Some parents elect to pour a panful of water over the child's head while the child's eyes are closed. Unfortunately, it is hard for two-year olds to keep their eyes closed when they are frightened, and this technique usually frightens them. One parent we interviewed, though, has poured water over her son's head during every bath since he was an infant, and in this case the technique was successful. Other parents encourage children from an early age to take showers, in the hope that they will not be afraid of water in their eyes. This approach can be successful, especially if the parent takes showers with the child and gives the child plenty of time to play around the edges of the spray before going in. The children can be given additional control over the water by using a hand spray. Again, however, the difficulty arises when children with soapy hair open their eyes in the shower and the soapy water runs into their eyes.

The best strategy, in our opinion, is to develop a routine that keeps the child's head stationary and in a position so that shampoo can be rinsed toward the back of the head. For example, if parents have a sink with an adjacent counter, the two-year old can lie down (face up) on the counter, while the parent holds the child's head over the sink. Using a washrag, the parent can then rinse the shampoo from the front of the child's head toward the back.

The same technique can be used in the bathtub by putting only an inch or two of water in the bottom. The child then lies down in the bathtub and the rinsing takes place. One parent we visited found she could position her child's head properly by giving the child a bubble pipe and telling the child to blow bubbles toward the ceiling. As the child looked up to watch the bubbles fly, the parent applied the rinse water.

The key to hair washing with two-year olds is to find some procedure that relaxes them. If children are relaxed in the shower, or when a panful of water is dumped over them in the bathtub, it will not be too difficult for them to learn to keep their eyes closed until all the soap is gone. If children can relax lying down in a few inches of water in the bathtub, or on a counter, the rinsing problem is solved. Learning to relax in a potentially frightening situation takes time. When children have developed a fear of hair washing, or of water in their eyes, parents need to realize that any technique will require patience on their part. Invariably, however, the children will one day be bursting with pride because they have learned to wash their hair without one bit of crying.

Housework

Kelly's grandmother had invited the family to brunch. "Do you suppose you could be finished with the housework in an hour and get over early?" Grandma asked. "I think so," Kelly's mother answered, "as long as Kelly doesn't decide she would like to help me."

Most two-year olds really enjoy helping with the housework. The favorite things to help with, of course, are usually those items with which the parent least wants help. Children love to wash dishes, water plants, or disperse the cleaning sprays. Despite this complication, some of the families we visited were quite successful at capitalizing on their two-year old's desire to help out. Jon's mother took the extra time to teach Jon how to water plants without drowning them, and how to wash dishes without simultaneously washing the floor. She found that Jon was a genuine help with the housework and was even able to push the vacuum cleaner around.

The major issue concerning housework was picking up. Parents differed greatly in their expectations. Some parents expected children to be responsible for picking up their own toys from the age of eighteen months on; others thought that four years old was about the right age. Most of the families felt that two-year olds should participate to some extent in picking up.

Looking more closely at the conflict over picking up, it appeared that the

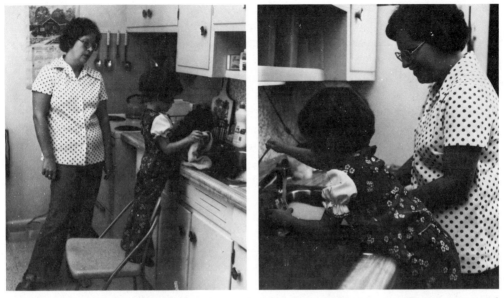

real issue was the use of toys in certain parts of the house. Toys scattered in a child's bedroom were not too upsetting. It was the mess in the family room, or the clutter in the kitchen, that caused most of the trouble. Of course, children transport their toys to the "living" rooms of the house as soon as they begin to walk (or even crawl). But it seems that between the ages of two and three, many parents hope this situation will change.

One reason for expecting change is that the children are able to play more independently, which suggests that they might play independently in a bedroom. Another reason is that the children are better able to understand explanations, which leads parents to think that they should be able to understand why picking up is necessary. A third reason is that the patience of parents simply gives out. They get tired of the clutter and decide they have put up with it long enough.

In the strictest households we visited, parents tried to enforce the rule that children get out only one thing at a time. When they were finished playing with that toy, it was to be put back before getting out another. Some parents commented that their children were trained to play with one thing at a time in nursery school, so why not do the same at home? This rule was more a vision in the minds of parents than a reality. We visited only one home in which the child really practiced what the parent preached, and this home was run very much like a school. In other cases the rule led to continual conflict. Apparently the children saw their homes as being different from a school environment and they were unwilling to accept the same rules.

Most families aimed for one or two general cleanups a day. This practice was successful if parents helped. If they tried to force children to pick up on their own, a slowdown, or even a sitdown, was likely. This suggests to us that two year old children do not really accept the need for picking up, but if it is part of a pleasant social experience, they are happy to participate.

When parents help pick up, it also makes the activity like an adult job. Participating in an adult activity is much more likely to appeal to a two-year old's sense of autonomy. Several families had provided toy boxes or baskets in the living room. In this way, toys could be picked up without taking them to the bedroom. This idea makes picking up more convenient, and it also may make it more important in the eyes of a child. From a child's viewpoint, taking toys to the bedroom may seem almost insulting. These toys are precious possessions and they are being excluded from the important parts of the house.

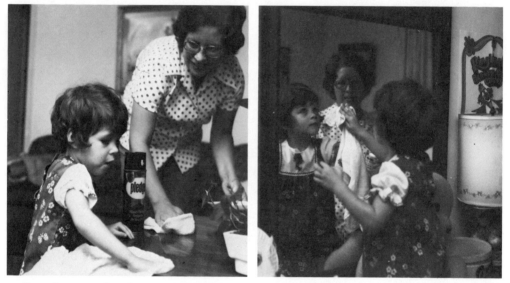

A toybox or a basket encourages picking up because it is fun to throw things in. In the long run, however, it discourages order because it is hard to find anything without emptying the whole box. The most easily understood reason for picking up is that it keeps toys from getting lost or misplaced. Two-year olds readily understand this principle with individual toys. They enjoy finding the pieces and fitting them together. But when the toys are then piled in a toybox, the purpose for picking up becomes obscure.

An alternative that seems especially good for two-year olds is a shallow cabinet; that is, a set of narrow shelves with a door. Opening and closing the door makes the cabinet an exciting container, while the shelves allow the child to find individual toys easily. For parents who are very intent on teaching a two-year old to pick up, we would recommend building or buying such a cabinet for the family room, kitchen, or wherever the child plays most often.

Regardless of how ingenious or persistent parents are, most two-year olds will continue to see picking up as a social activity. They will not be very interested in doing the job by themselves. Parents may think that only a few weeks, or months, of picking up with the children will be sufficient to model this behavior. Our experience indicates, however, that it takes a much longer time for children to internalize the value of a tidy room. It is reasonable to introduce the idea of picking up at this age, but it is unrealistic to expect the lesson to be fully learned.

*   *   *

In this chapter we have discussed some solutions to problems involved in sleeping, eating, dressing, and cleaning up. Many other possibilities exist, however. A good way for parents to generate new ideas is to think about how conflict can be avoided. Can the rules be made more consistent? Is there a way to distract a child, to defuse the problem by using humor and imagination? Can the child participate in a substitute activity? The size of a family affects the tactics that are chosen. A larger family must be better organized, which means that planning ahead, setting rules, and giving clear explanations are especially valuable. A small family, on the other hand, has more opportunity to handle routines through distraction, imaginative rituals, and compromise.

In discussing daily routines we have glossed over the non-routine events that happen nearly every day. These unusual events often are less private. Either the family goes out in public or other people come into the home. Because the experiences are out of the ordinary, the children become extra excited. This higher level of excitement, combined with the public character of unusual events, makes conflict more likely to occur and more difficult to resolve.

Parents do not have the same range of options. They have less time to explain, are too busy or embarrassed to play games, and it is harder to compromise. Often they cannot discipline children by applying logical consequences, using isolation, or depriving them of privileges. This dilemma is an occupational hazard for parents of two-year olds, to be accepted with as much grace as possible. Parents should not, of course, avoid outings, but neither should they overreact when children misbehave. We observed the following incident while writing this book. It is typical of the kind of overreaction that can be seen every day in restaurants, grocery stores and other public places.

A two-year old was sitting in an ice cream parlor with his older sister and parents. The two-year old put his hand on the table and began to finger his mother's spoon. She slapped his hand without looking down and continued talking with her husband. Several minutes later the boy fingered her spoon again. This time the mother picked up the spoon and hit him across the fingers. Just at that moment the waitress arrived with a tray full of ice cream sundaes. The mother stuck a spoon in the boy's ice cream and told him to go ahead and eat. The child stared at the spoon with frightened eyes and never touched the ice cream.

Whether they are in public or at home, parents want their children to be obedient. Two-year olds, on the other hand, focus on ways to expand their sense of autonomy. This difference in perspective leads to conflict over daily routines. In many instances parent-child conflict has positive outcomes. It results in compromise and greater communication between parents and children. Because conflict is rooted in the different roles of parents and children, however, it continues to exist.

If conflict is an inevitable part of daily routines, so is the joy of living together. As we watch families with two-year olds handle the problems and enjoy the benefits of everyday living, we realize that there is no one best child rearing style. In fact, each family comes to recognize that every child—and every family—is different. Techniques that work well with one child are not right for another. Ultimately, parent effectiveness depends on being sensitive to the unique characteristics of individual children.

Chapter 3
MAKING FRIENDS

In many traditional books on child development, the social play of the two-year old is described as "parallel." In parallel play, children play alongside each other, aware of each other's presence but not really interacting. This may be an apt description of the play behavior of some two-year olds, but it does not tell the whole story. Many children even younger than two-years old have already learned to enjoy peer interaction and can play cooperatively for short bits of time. Certainly between the ages of two and three we see the emergence of social skills in peer play. In addition, many two-year olds are learning to interact with siblings. In this chapter we will look at three situations for learning social skills: adjusting to a new baby, playing with older siblings, and playing with friends.

Living With Siblings

Parents who have developed a close relationship with their first child are usually quite concerned when a new baby is expected. They are prepared for all the symptoms of sibling rivalry—anger, jealousy, pouting, purposeful naughtiness, demanding behavior, and regression. There are many simple activities in which parents may engage their two-year olds to ease their transition to big sisterhood or big brotherhood, and to pave the way for friendly sibling relations.

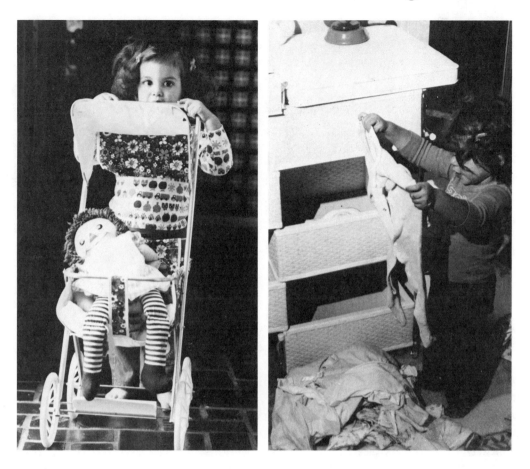

Before the Baby Is Born

Use the months ahead to help your two-year old develop an understanding of "new babies" and a feeling of the importance of being a "big brother" or "sister."

1. When the baby is active enough, give your two-year old an opportunity to feel your stomach. Make sure to say, "Feel the baby stretching," or "Feel the baby moving." Two-year olds may not like the idea of a baby kicking Mommy.

2. Go through the baby book and show your two-year old the pictures of when she (or he) was a baby. Talk about how little she was, and how she could not sit or walk or even feed herself.

3. Sort through your two-year old's baby clothes. Talk about how little she was when she was a baby. Together choose the clothes that will fit the new

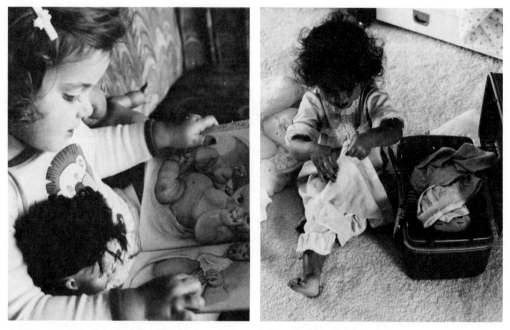

baby soon after birth. Your two-year old will get a feeling for how little the baby will be.

4. Talk to your two-year old about all the things the baby will be using: a crib, a carriage, a baby bath, and perhaps a cradle. Don't be surprised if your two-year old wants to try things out.

5. Help your two-year old take care of a baby doll. You can introduce the idea slowly that babies need lots of time and care. Let her give her doll a bath in the new baby's tub. This will be a good time to talk about how gentle you have to be with a new baby.

6. Let your two-year old take part in your exercises. This time together gives you a chance to talk in a casual way about your new baby's birth.

7. You and your two-year old can make something together for the new baby. Choose something simple and easy to complete, like a quiet sign or a picture to go over the crib.

8. Teach your two-year old a lullaby to sing to her new baby. This will help her know that she will be an important helper when the new baby is born.

9. You and your two-year old can plan the new baby's room together. Then take her on a shopping trip to buy some items for the new baby.

10. Give your two-year old a turn rocking in your arms in the new baby's rocking chair. Talk about how sometimes it's fun to be a big sister and sometimes it's fun to pretend to be a baby.

11. If you are planning to breast feed, invite a friend over who is breast feeding her baby. Your two-year old will adjust more easily if she knows what to

expect.

12. In preparation for the baby's homecoming, let your two-year old choose the outfit that the baby will wear home from the hospital. Your two-year old will enjoy discovering how her baby looks in the clothes she selected.

13. Drive to the hospital with your two-year old. She will make a better adjustment to your going to the hospital if she knows where you are going to be.

When the Baby Is Born

1. Several weeks before the baby is due, begin to discuss the fact that soon Mommy and Daddy will be going to the hospital to bring the new baby home. Tell your two-year old who will be coming to take care of her and describe the special things she will be doing while Mommy is in the hospital. If your two-year old is staying at a relative's house, let her be involved in packing her suitcase for the trip. Also, let your two-year old help you pack your suitcase. It will help her understand that you won't be away for long.

2. Bring a polaroid camera to the hospital so you can send a picture of the new baby home with Daddy.

3. If your two-year old enjoys phone conversations, call her from the hospital to tell her about the new baby.

4. Have a special big sister or big brother present ready to give your two-year old when the baby comes home. This may be a special baby doll for

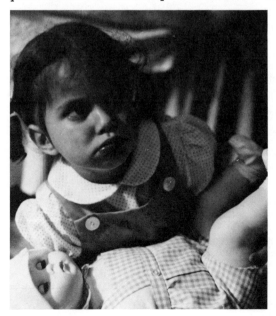
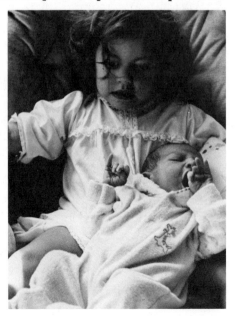

your two-year old to take care of.

5. Let Daddy carry the new baby into the house so Mommy's arms will be free to hug the new big sister. Together you can go to meet the new baby.

6. Explain in advance the "rules" for holding the new baby. The rules may be that you have to be sitting in a chair, that you need to hold the baby's head and that the baby goes back to Mommy when he starts to cry.

7. Have a home-coming party for the new baby. Since the baby is not old enough to eat cake, your two-year old will have to eat it for him.

8. Read stories with your two-year old about being a big sister or big brother. Choose books that will help your two-year old cope with feelings of jealousy.

Adjusting to a New Baby

Two-year olds usually are pleased with the arrival of a baby brother or sister, especially when parents have prepared them for the new family member. They enjoy sorting laundry and bringing in diapers. (Many of the children are just mastering the toilet and are pleased when the baby messes.) When not helping Mommy or Daddy take care of the baby, two-year olds are likely to tend their own dolls and stuffed animals. Dolls that have spent months in the bottom of a toy chest are resurrected and pressed into service.

This honeymoon period may not last long. After a while, two-year olds recognize that a new baby gets a special kind of attention. Adults are constantly vying for a chance to hold the baby and the baby's every move is admired from all sides. Just when the parents have relaxed their fear of sibling rivalry, the dreaded symptoms appear. Alesha's mother's account is fairly typical. "At first when the baby was born everything was peaches and cream, but just recently I'm seeing signs of jealousy. As soon as I begin to breast-feed the baby, Alesha starts with, 'I got to go to potty, hurry up!'" In contrast to Alesha, Chad was forthright about his feelings toward his brother. "I don't like my brother," he informed his parents, "because you are always holding him." When Chad's mother sang to the baby, "You are so beautiful," Chad voiced his protest. "Sing that song to me. Don't sing that to my brother."

In some cases parents may be able to modify or tone down the special attention a new baby receives. Brian's parents, for example, discovered that Brian was jealous of the way they took care of the baby at night. Brian and the baby shared a room, and the parents were very attentive to the baby whenever he cried out. Brian tried crying out too, but he didn't get the same kind of attention. This source of jealousy was removed by simply moving the baby to another room. After that, Brian slept through the night.

Another way to help two-year olds cope with their jealousy is to allow them to participate in intimate interaction with the baby. Greg's mother showed him how he could hold his baby sister's hand while she was drinking her bottle. Mary's mother taught her to play with the baby's feet instead of investigating his face.

Nothing quite equals the smiling and cooing of a young baby, and two-year olds, like adults, can be captivated by the baby's responsiveness. Furthermore, two-year olds have a natural ability to entertain babies. We observed several children playing with baby brothers and sisters in a crib or playpen. In these places the usual relationships were reversed. The two-year old took the lead in interacting with the baby and became the prime object of the baby's attention, while the parents watched from the sidelines.

Finally, parents can try to communicate to their two-year olds that there are advantages in being the most "grown-up" child in a family. Mary's mother, for example, reminded Mary that she could move around, run and jump, while the baby just had to lie on his back. Mary could drink from a cup and could even choose what to eat, while the baby always had to eat the same thing. The most dramatic way to demonstrate this idea is to take the two-year old on a special outing—without the baby. The outing can be very simple, because the idea of having special time is more important than the activity. One of Brian's favorite activities, for example, was to go around the corner and have breakfast with his mother.

Keeping Up With Older Siblings

Many of the families we visited were concerned about the feelings of jealousy between two-year olds and older siblings. The two-year olds tried to emulate their older brothers and sisters. They felt able to do the same things and they expected the same privileges. Parents found themselves, on the one hand, encouraging two-year olds to develop new skills, but on the other hand trying to convince them that equal treatment was not always possible. In dealing with the older siblings, the parents were caught in a similar dilemma. They wanted to support the rights of the older children but at the same time tried to persuade them that a two-year old needs plenty of breathing room in order to grow.

A two-year old's feelings of sibling rivalry may be expressed in exaggerated "me too" behavior. Willie, who was just barely two, was watching his older sister Susan chewing gum. Willie didn't really know what gum was and was quite happy with the wrapper Susan gave him. He popped the wrapper in his mouth and started chewing. Apparently it didn't taste very good and the family giggled at his expression of surprise and disgust. However, Willie's demands for similar treatment continued and, after a while they stopped being funny. When Susan was given penicillin for an ear infection,

Willie wanted his penicillin, too. When Susan put on a yellow dress for Sunday School, Willie cried bitterly until his mother let him wear a dress.

Another common way of expressing rivalry is learning to become a tease. Christopher, the youngest of three children, was a master of this strategy. While we were visiting, he knocked down his sister's block building in a quick commando raid. Next he ran into the bedroom to retrieve and then hide his brother's favorite stuffed dog.

Still another way two-year olds attempt to protect their "turf" is to demand more attention from their parents. When Jodi's older sister was showing her kindergarten papers, Jodi kept tugging at her mother's skirt and insisting, "I have something to tell you." Nicole's strategy was to appeal to her mother's sympathies. "Little Nicole is very sad because you won't pick me up. Little Nicole is a baby." Bernie had decided that if he couldn't get his fair share of attention by being good, he would certainly get it by being bad. As soon as his father began playing with his older brother, he deliberately sought out every naughty activity he could think of.

If these tactics are ineffective, two-year olds may directly attack their older siblings. They may break a brother's or sister's treasured possession. They may echo back the taunts of older children. "I don't like you. I won't even play with you. I won't be your friend." They may resort to biting, scratching, pinching, or throwing things.

Between two and three years of age, a child's confrontations with older siblings are likely to intensify. Battles over possessions, privileges and status in the family are continually rocking the household. From the point of view of parents, the most ridiculous things can create the biggest ruckus. Who is going to sit in the brown chair in front of the television set? Who gets the rose on the icing of the birthday cake? Who turns the pages in the "Goodnight Moon" story book?

Parents naturally feel badly about these signs of sibling rivalry and, inevitably, they blame themselves. Although this kind of self-blame is un-

derstandable, it certainly is not warranted. Actually sibling rivalry is a good sign. It shows that the children value the time and attention of their parents. We found, in fact, that sibling rivalry was most intense in child-oriented families. In families where parents were punitive or aloof, siblings had much less reason to compete with each other.

Ways of Responding to Sibling Rivalry

Every family develops its own philosophy for handling the rivalry between two-year olds and older siblings. Some parents feel that it is their responsiblity to intervene in sibling fights and teach the children how to get along. Timothy's mother, for example, was a firm believer in settling differences by talking about them. "If I stand there and let them fight, I am actually condoning fighting. I am saying to them, 'Go ahead, fight it out, might makes right.' No, sir. I tell my children that we talk over problems with our mouths, not our fists, and you know, even my two-year old understands." When Timothy's sister borrowed his security blanket to cover her doll, Timothy came running into the room tumbling over his words, "Allison, my blanket—Allison took it, my blanket—talk about it Mommy."

Other families adopt a hands-off policy toward sibling rivalry. They believe that children will resolve their differences sooner or later if left alone. Chris' father put it this way: "You can't pull kids apart every time they get into a fight. It's a tough world out there and they have to learn to stand up for themselves. I tell my wife, 'Don't ever pull the kids apart unless you see blood.'"

In most cases, families find themselves somewhere in between these two extremes. They try to diffuse sibling rivalry, but without actually intervening and requiring the children to behave in a certain way. One family, for example, tried to turn potential conflicts into playful situations. When Bennie insisted that his cookie was smaller than Annie's, their mother responded by saying that she would feed Bennie's cookie some vitamins so that it would grow as big as Annie's. Although this kind of humor may go over the children's heads, the cheerful parental tone is catching.

Most families also make a conscious effort to communicate to their children that they are loved equally. One approach with young children is to establish a special time for each child to interact with parents. This is a common practice at bedtime. The children go to bed at different times and each one gets a story or some form of special attention before going to sleep. We visited one family who had carried this idea much further and felt happy with it. Michael, the two-year old, had "his time" with mother during a specified period of the day while the two older children were at school. Shawn, who was in kindergarten, came home at two o'clock and "her time" extended for the next half hour. Later in the afternoon Billy, the eight-year old, received "his time."

Lisa and Jeffrey's mother took a different approach. Instead of giving her children separate attention, she planned special activities that the children could do alongside each other. One day both children might put together puzzles, each doing his own puzzle on his own brightly decorated orange crate table. The next day they might do a coloring project or play with clay. This technique required a lot of planning but, based on our observation, it worked well. Naturally, competition and rivalry still existed. Lisa, who certainly sensed her coloring skills were not equal to those of her four year old brother, told us as she finished a drawing, "I go slow so I can make mine more pretty."

One of the most common methods for communicating equal consideration is to make sure that siblings take turns enjoying a special privilege. At Marcie's house, for example, the children fought over saying the prayer before meals. The most sensible solution was to take turns, even though Marcie's prayers did not make as much sense as her older brothers'. Sometimes a

simple chart helps keep track of whose turn it is. Heath, Colby, and Jeff all wanted to go grocery shopping with their father, who was not home very much. Three at a time was too much, so a chart was set up to indicate whose turn it was to accompany Daddy to the store. A timer also may be appropriate for teaching children to take turns. Krista fought with her ten year old brother over who would get to sit in Daddy's chair to watch television. The problem was solved, or at least reduced in intensity, by setting a timer for ten minutes and letting the children switch seats at the sound of the bell.

It may seem contradictory to communicate equal love by punishing children, but most parents at some point find themselves trying to stop sibling rivalry in this way. One technique is to take away the toys that the children are fighting over. This is a logical step but does not seem to be too successful with a two-year old, who can easily find another reason to fight if so inclined. Many parents reported that the best solution was to separate the children. This punishment is also logical as it communicates to children that, if they cannot get along, they cannot play together. As Lori and Lisa's mother told us, "My girls can do without a specific toy, but it is harder to do without a companion. Within five minutes they have usually sneaked out of their rooms and are playing together quietly so I won't hear them."

It would be nice to be able to present families with the one best answer for "curing" sibling rivalry. However, as is always true in child rearing, there are no easy answers. Each family must work out a solution that is right for them. In the long run, the best way to reduce sibling rivalry is to encourage sibling cooperation. Jeffrey, who was four years old, had recently enlisted his two year old sister, Lisa, as an ally. Together they explored the closets and hid behind the curtains. Jeffrey turned the lights off and then they got under the sheet and made monster and ghost noises. "Scary, Mommy?" Lisa would ask. Although their mother was not always enthusiastic about these joint endeavors, she tolerated them because they fostered a feeling of comraderie

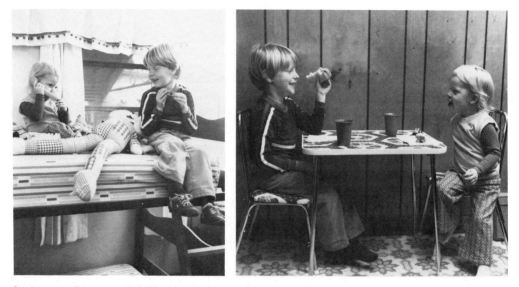

between Lisa and Jeffrey.

We observed a similar pattern between Kelly and her five year old brother, Kyle. They played happily in their room, making a huge pile of toys on the upper bunk bed. When it was time to wash up for lunch, they enjoyed splashing water on each other. At lunchtime, they sat at a little table in the kitchen while their mother cleaned the house. Instead of eating, they pushed the table back and forth, grabbed food from each other's plates and spilled their glasses of milk. The children may have been fighting, as their mother thought, but it seemed more likely to us that they had formed an alliance for the specific purpose of tormenting her.

Sibling cooperation, as well as sibling rivalry, can have its drawbacks. Yet it is important to focus on the real advantages in being part of a family with more than one child. The child from a larger family has a twenty-four hour on-call playmate. This playmate is a source of stimulation, companionship and even protection. Many parents who complained about children fighting with each other on the homefront told us that, when other children were around, the older sibling watched over and protected the two-year old. Being part of a larger family means increased social experience as well. Two-year olds with older siblings learn how to initiate contact with other children, how to ignore minor hurts and falls, how to talk and joke with peers, and how to share the same toys. Having learned these social skills at home with brothers and sisters, it is easier to function in new situations with other children.

Playing With Friends

Having an Older Friend

Two-year olds are usually at a perfect age for playing with older children. They are so happy with the idea of being included in the older child's play that they take on any role that is assigned. In an imaginative play situation they are content to be the baby or the patient. When the other children are quite a lot older, imaginative play progresses even more smoothly. Krista, for example, had a well defined role in her ten year old brother's peer group. While the older children pretended to be a brass band, Krista danced and sang. Being less inhibited, she was ideal for the part.

Play with older children is not limited to imaginative play. When there are older children to play with, a two-year old enjoys chase games, hide and seek activities, tumbling, tricycle riding, and any kind of jumping or climbing activities. The fact that the two-year old is less adept amuses the older child and doesn't seem to bother the younger one. The two-year old, for instance, may be so delighted to be riding a wheel toy with his big friend that he doesn't mind the fact that his friend covers twice the distance in half the time.

Naturally, there are occasions when play breaks down between older and

younger children. This is most apt to happen if an older child takes possession of a toy and completely ignores the two-year old. Many manipulative toys are not designed to encourage cooperation. A battery-operated helicopter, for example, only needs one "pilot." A two-year old may be satisfied playing with an inexpensive plastic airplane while the older child runs the fancy helicopter. When imitation is not possible, however, and cooperation is not needed, a two-year old is likely to be left out.

Some of the parents we visited did express concern over bad habits that their two-year olds picked up from older children. One type of bad habit was name-calling or unkind remarks, such as, "I don't like you. You're not my friend." In the same vein, several parents mentioned that their children had started using words like "hate," "stupid," "dummy," and "baby." These are fighting words among children and become useful to the young child who is trying to substitute words for hitting and biting. Although parents are upset to hear them, they indicate that a child is progressing from physical violence to verbal aggression. Actually this concern about name calling is more characteristic of parents who do not have older children. In families with older siblings, verbal assaults may be so commonplace that parents hardly notice when the two-year old joins in.

The other kind of bad habit that parents described was "cursing." Two-year olds are just beginning to appreciate the attention to be gained by repeating unmentionable words. For the most part, these "bad words" are innocent "pooh-poohs" and "pee-pees." In Michael's neighborhood, the parents were trying to squelch this kind of talk, so instead of yelling "pooh-pooh" and "pee-pee," the children hollered "conch" and "duey" which, of course, meant pooh-pooh and pee-pee to anyone in the know.

We know of no quick solution to this problem. The "bad words" of two-year olds are more tiresome than nasty. They are a sign to parents that the power of the peer group is growing and that, in some instances, its influence exceeds their own. The best advice we can offer parents is to keep their sense of humor and to try not to be annoyed.

The negatives that parents talked about were more than outweighed by the positive effects of having their two-year olds play with older children. Because two-year olds are great imitators, an older child can serve not only as a playmate but also as a most effective teacher. Ginny's mother had spent many fruitless hours trying to teach Ginny how to put on her socks. Ginny resisted the lesson. "Socks too hard, Mommy. Ginny's a little baby." One day her three year old cousin, Barbara, spent the night. Ginny's mother was surprised the next morning when she went into the room to find Ginny on the end of the bed with both her socks on. "Did you help Ginny with her socks?" she asked Barbara. "I putted mine on and Ginny putted hers on," Barbara answered matter-of-factly.

Playing With Another Two-Year Old

When children play with their same-age peers, the play sessions are usually less smooth than they are with older children. One of the big bug-a-boos here is sharing toys. Two-year olds have just gotten a firm handle on the concept of possessions. They recognize that each member of the family has certain things that belong just to them. These facts frequently are reflected in the language of two-year olds: "your briefcase," "my teddy bear," "Daddy's keys."

Being told to share possessions is a puzzling kind of request. Why do you have to share something if it really belongs to you? Parents often urge their children to share because other children have shared with them. But how often is this true? From a two-year old's perspective, other children frequently do not share, and they give every indication of wanting to keep the toys they are playing with. As adults we know that a borrowed toy eventually will be returned to its original owner, but how do two-year olds know that a toy will still belong to them if they agree to share it? The idea that possession is nine-tenths of the law must seem a very compelling argument to a young child.

Here again we see the difference between only children and those with siblings. In a family with several children it is common to consider many of the toys joint property. This gives the children more experience in sharing and they are therefore more likely to share their toys with friends. The difference is only one of degree, however. In almost every family, there are special toys that are the exclusive property of individual children. Brothers and sisters are not allowed to play with these special toys unless they have the owner's specific permission. When we visited John, for example, he grudgingly allowed his sister to play with several of the toys in his room, but she absolutely could not sit on his new motorcycle.

Between the ages of two and three, many children learn to share their toys with certain friends in certain circumstances. However, it is not unusual for possessiveness to actually increase during this year. As children have more contact with peers, their reaction may be to guard possessions even more closely. They may begin to covet the possessions of others. Being able to share represents a feeling of trust, and it takes some children longer to extend this trust to their peers. Again it should be emphasized that every situation is different. Children's attitudes toward sharing are affected by whose home they are in, how long they have known the other child, the personality and age of the other child, and what toy is at issue.

Even when children have progressed to the point of sharing their toys, it often happens that the toy being requested is not a toy they are willing to share. Kori discussed this dilemma with her mother in a tearful conversation:

Kori: "I don't want Jason to take my Snoopy. Jason play with my Snoopy too long. Jason can play with my harmonica."

Mother: "Yes, that's a good idea. You can bring Jason your harmonica."

Kori: "Jason don't want my harmonica. Jason can play with my bubbles."

Mother: "That's a fine idea."

Kori: "Jason don't want my bubbles. I don't want to share Snoopy. I can share Snoopy with Molly. Molly gives my toys back."

As children turn three, they are more likely to demonstrate selective selfishness. They now realize that one way to hurt another person is to deprive that person of a certain possession or privilege. Andy did not want one of the neighborhood boys to be allowed in his pool, and at his birthday party he told his mother that one particular girl "doesn't like cake."

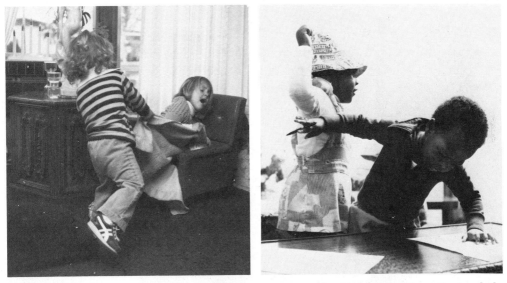

The parents we visited were quite concerned about teaching their children to share. The rule most frequently used by parents was that whoever got a toy first had the right to keep it. This rule is crude, but it does communicate that grabbing a toy out of someone else's hand is wrong.

Sooner or later most parents try to explain why it is not nice to grab a toy. These explanations generally don't make much of an impression, judging from the dull look they inspire on the child's face. A two-year old needs a concrete verbal formulation to understand the significance of the explanation.

Mary's mother seemed to have hit on a good idea. When a fight broke out over a toy, she tried to find out who the trespasser was by referring to him as the grouch. "Who's the grouch now? Bev, you're the grouch—Robbie already had the cement mixer. Come on, grouch. Let's find you another toy." The children soon learned how the identity of the grouch was determined and that everyone was the grouch at one time or another. The verbal ritual of being labeled the grouch communicated, in a nonpunitive way, one of the basic rules of sharing.

Mary's mother had introduced another verbal formula that facilitated sharing at an early age. At the dinner table, food often was divided and distributed by saying, "One for Mary, one for Mommy, and one for Daddy." This formula was repeated in diverse settings, such as rolling a ball back and forth and saying, "One for Mommy . . . one for Mary." By the age of two, Mary had shown interest in dividing her toys among her friends in the same way. The magic of counting helped her overcome the tendency to hoard possessions.

Matthew's mother suggested another technique fo facilitate sharing. Many families allow children to take one toy along when they go out. This toy can be used in the car and also at a friend's house. Matthew's mother reversed the idea. She taught Matthew to take one of his toys just for the friend to play with. In this way, Matthew was able to initiate the sharing by offering a toy to the host child, rather than the usual procedure of waiting for the largess

of the host to materialize. Imagine how much less threatened host children must feel when their guest immediately gives them a new toy to play with. The idea is comparable to bringing flowers or wine when invited to dinner, a token of gratitude in advance.

Terri's mother was very fond of having children come to play. Her strategy was to involve the children in a game or activity where sharing was less likely to be a problem. Frequently she introduced some sort of craft or cooking activity in which the children could cooperate. At other times she encouraged activities in which the children could imitate each other. The most successful activities were highly physical. The house had a large screened-in porch, directly off the kitchen, that could be filled with appropriate equipment. Some days she placed a wading pool on the porch and let the children play in the water. Other days she invited the children to bring their tricycles. Her favorite setup was an extra mattress, several cartons of different sizes, and some old sheets, blankets and pillows. The children climbed in and out of the cartons, jumped on the mattress and pillows, crawled under the sheets and blankets, and generally had a wild time.

Parents sometimes are concerned about the wild behavior of a two-year old peer group. Even when only two children get together, their play can appear to be regressive. Adele had gone beyond the stage of pulling everything off the shelves and her room stayed reasonably neat. When her friend, Yvonne, came over to play, Adele's mother thought it would be all right to let the children play by themselves in Adele's bedroom. She was thoroughly dismayed, however, when she walked into the room several minutes later and found the place in shambles. All the toys were out of the toy box, books off the shelf, clothes out of the drawers and even the bed clothes were off the bed.

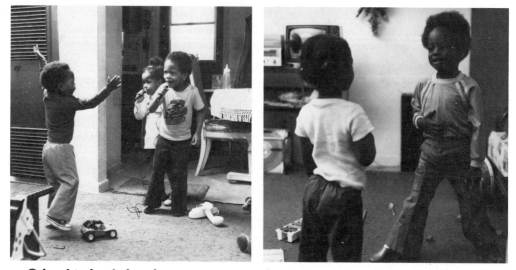

Other kinds of play that parents consider regressive include chasing games, snatch-away-the-toy games, shouting, throwing things, raucous laughter, and knocking all sorts of things over. It probably is a mistake to consider this type of spontaneous interaction between two-year olds as regressive play. What is happening is that the two-year olds are attempting to involve each other in a game. They are not sophisticated enough to think up a complicated game so they rely on activities that are guaranteed to produce social interaction.

Organizing peer play requires both responsible leaders and responsive followers. Two-year olds do not fit easily into either role. The dominant children have trouble communicating their plans and are basically tyrannical. The more passive children have trouble seeing any sense in the largely unintelligible plans of the "leaders," and are expert at sabotaging these plans by teasing or withdrawing. Under these circumstances, physical games of imitation are a natural peer group activity. They require little sharing and almost no social organization.

Styles of Playing

Each child's personality and play style is unique but, in general, children between the ages of two and three begin to define their style of playing with peers by transferring the style they have developed within the family. It is common for first-born children to be somewhat domineering, especially if their parents are the kind who reason and compromise with them. These children are used to having their ideas treated with respect within the family and they expect peers to do the same. We visited several families in which first-born children between two and one half and three years were trying to direct three and four year old children. Michael, for example, organized the peer group's imaginative play around a hospital theme, casting himself in the principal role. He became upset if the neighbor children wanted to play by themselves instead of playing with him. Beverly assumed her mother's role of helping the peer group do arts and crafts projects. Her mother was proud of Beverly's leadership ability but cringed at her bossiness: "Don't color that way, Lisa . . . All right, time to stop coloring . . . Put your crayons away right now."

Of course, later-born children can develop domineering play styles as well. We found families in which the second child had been encouraged to be more assertive because the parents had changed their minds about discipline. They felt they had been too strict with their first child and so were allowing the second child more leeway to argue with them and to stretch the rules.

Whether children tend to be bossy, teasing, or passive, their social skills grow as they gain more experience with the peer group. Twins or other children who have spent a lot of time playing with peers may display considerable sophistication. Two year old Rocheda, for example, demonstrated an impressive degree of versatility during our visit to her house. Her mother took out the vacuum cleaner so that we could see how well Rocheda had learned to push it around. Her cousin, Eddie, however, was also interested in the vacuum cleaner and managed to get to it first. Rocheda tried to retrieve the vacuum cleaner with a polite request. That didn't work. Next, she tried a kiss — still no success. Finally, she gave her cousin a good shove and yanked the vacuum out of his hand.

Although children differ in their play styles, there seems to be a common pattern in the evolution of peer group relationships. In a new peer group, the two-year old tends to be passive. The child takes the role of onlooker, imitator and follower. During this phase, parents may be distressed that their child is being pushed around. Jenny's mother told us, "Jenny is the smallest child in the neighborhood, and the other kids were always hitting her and taking away her toys. Finally I had to tell her to hit them back."

As the new children become more comfortable in the peer group, they begin to assert themselves. They may become unusually assertive, just as they were unusually passive earlier. Jenny's mother related that after Jenny started asserting her rights, there was a constant struggle over toys. She found it necessary to intervene continually when two or three friends were playing in Jenny's room.

Eventually some kind of balance is struck as the members of the group develop a stable pattern of interaction. In the case of Jenny's peer group, it took about three months. Parents play an important role in helping children progress through this sequence. They can avoid overreacting when the child

appears either too timid or too aggressive. At the same time, however, they can keep a watchful eye on the situation, offering suggestions or guidance when they feel it is necessary. Most importantly, they can be interested and sympathetic, willing to listen and respond to the outbursts of joy, apprehension, and frustration that peer group experience produces in a two-year old.

As in other aspects of child rearing, parents need to recognize that children are different and do not all need the same kinds of social experiences. Some children simply enjoy watching from the sidelines, or playing alongside another child, but do not want to join in the noisy activity of the peer group. At a birthday party, Lori, who is basically a gentle, non-aggressive child, retreated into a corner and played quietly until the party ended. "I don't want a lot of screaming kids at my birthday party," she informed her mother.

Group Experience

Many families must put their young children in a child care facility because there is no adult at home during the day to take care of them. Other families choose to send two-year olds to nursery school or a play group because they feel the children need the experience. We found that the parents we visited expressed two contrasting points of view about the best environment for children between the ages of two and three. According to one school of thought, two-year olds are too young for directed activity and should be allowed to spend their time in a relaxed climate playing with toys and exploring the things around them. The role of the adult is primarily to make certain that the children are safe and happy. The contrasting philosophy is based on the belief that two-year olds are ready for a more structured environment and can benefit from carefully planned experiences and direct teaching.

It seems to us that both these philosophies are valid. Two-year olds need a predictable environment in which they feel emotionally secure and are free to set their own direction and pace for learning. At the same time, two-year olds can benefit from a stimulating environment that is based on careful planning, specialized materials and exposure to a variety of children and adults. Ideally, group settings for young children should combine the qualities of both environments. They should offer the advantages of both a home and a school.

In our experience, however, many group child care facilities do not approach this ideal. They have neither the atmosphere of a good home nor the planning of a good school. Our impression is that this situation will not change until much greater resources are available to day care centers.

While visiting day care centers, we were impressed by the ability of the children to regulate their behavior in the classroom. The children were well adjusted to the large group setting. They sat quietly at tables waiting for instructions, went to the bathroom in an orderly fashion and ate their food with restraint. However, they did not seem very happy and, as soon as we tried to start an informal conversation or game with one child, we were inundated by other children seeking some of our attention. This frantic scramble for attention suggests that a highly structured situation does not meet the needs of a two-year old.

Some child care centers are more relaxed. Teacher directed activities are interspersed with extended periods of free play. The classroom is both spacious and well-equipped. Even under these favorable conditions, however, a large group setting is difficult for two-year olds. Several of the parents we visited reported that their two-year olds begged to go to school like their older siblings but, after having tried it, they wanted no more of it. Jodi's case was a bit extreme but not atypical. She insisted on going to school but as soon as her mother left, Jodi crawled out of the window in order to escape. Trying another school, Jodi's mother found that she had to carry Jodi kicking and screaming to the car every morning. At pick-up time, Jodi was all smiles and claimed to have had a fine day at school.

Jodi's case illustrates the fact that many two-year olds do want contact with other children. They want both the social experience and the feeling of expanding their horizons beyond the home. Her behavior also demonstrates, however, that a large group setting can be overwhelming for two-year olds who have been cared for in a home environment. In order to combine the qualities of home and school, we feel it is highly desirable to organize day care, nursery school, and other group experiences for two-year olds in terms of small groups. A small group might consist of five to ten children.

Additional features that are important in choosing a successful group setting for two-year olds include:

1. Adults working with the children should be loving, enthusiastic and energetic: They should have a good sense of timing and be able to suggest a new activity or change in locale before a crisis occurs. They should call all the children by name, bend down to their level when they speak with them, and talk with each child individually about the "important things," like what they are wearing, what is happening at home, or what they did yesterday. They should have the capacity to see what is going on in all four corners of the room simultaneously.

2. Physical space for different types of activities: There should be places for pretend play, for motor activities, and for constructing things, as well as a fenced-in area for outdoor play. The center should be equipped with safe and intact materials, with items such as wagons, rocking boats and face-to-face swings that encourage children to play together. Play materials should be within reach of the children.

3. Daily schedule providing time for free play and time for planned activity: The planned activities should be very short and simple, requiring little preparation and clean up time. Certain activities should be re-

peated on a daily basis to provide the children with a sense of time and sequence.

4. Parents as an integral part of program planning and as frequent visitors to the center.

5. At least one adult for every five children between the ages of two and three.

Whether the group setting is a day care center, a preschool, or a neighborhood playgroup, the principal benefit is an opportunity to develop social skills. It is important that the play activities be designed to encourage peer interaction. Here are some of our favorites for two-year olds:

Circle Time Songs

A record or cassette player with a good selection of sing-along or activity records is almost a must for a playgroup. By choosing a song to begin the day, a song for snack time and a song for closing time, play leaders provide children with a time frame that gives them a sense of security.

Gymnastics

Two-year olds are active, exuberant and energetic. They need a time and a place for vigorous physical activity. A queen-size mattress and a collection of pillows provides a perfect arena for group exercise time.

Play-Dough Roll

A "Make the Play-dough" project is a good way to introduce the benefits of cooperative play. The activity begins with mixing the dough (peanut butter, cooking oil and powdered milk). After everyone, including the leader, has had an opportunity to mix the dough, each child is given a portion to pound, roll, squeeze or shape into whatever form he chooses.

Rhythm Band

Two-year olds are not very sophisticated about music, but they do enjoy rhythms, and they can keep time with a beat. Round cereal boxes are ideal for making drums, while frozen juice containers with large beans inside work very nicely as shakers.

Peg Board

Although a peg board is essentially an individual play material, children enjoy filling peg boards as a group activity. Acoustic ceiling tiles can be cut up to make inexpensive peg boards, so that any child who chooses can be given a board to fill up.

Puppet Play

The two-year old response to puppet play is more enthusiastic than any other age bracket. If every child in the group is given a puppet, puppet play can be the catalyst for creative conversation.

Water, Water, Everywhere

Two-year olds enjoy a variety of water play activities, including washing up the snack table, bathing their dolls, washing and drying the tea party dishes, and washing down the tricycles and other riding toys.

Parachute Play—Ball Play

Using an ordinary bed sheet as a parachute, let the two-year olds sit in a circle holding onto a section of the sheet. As the music starts off, toss a nerf ball in the center of the sheet. The children can watch the nerf ball fly up and fall down as they "flap" the parachute in time to the music.

Discovery Walk

When weather and location permit, take your two-year olds on a discovery walk. Attach a wide piece of stick-tape to their wrists so that the treasures of the hunt can be kept safely on the tape. At the end of the walk, encourage children to share their collection of treasures.

Dress-Up Time

Dressing up together is a beginning step in cooperative play. In deference to the dressing skills of two-year olds, you may want to limit the costume selection to tee-shirts, hats, beads, and slip-on shoes.

Chapter 4
LEARNING THROUGH LANGUAGE

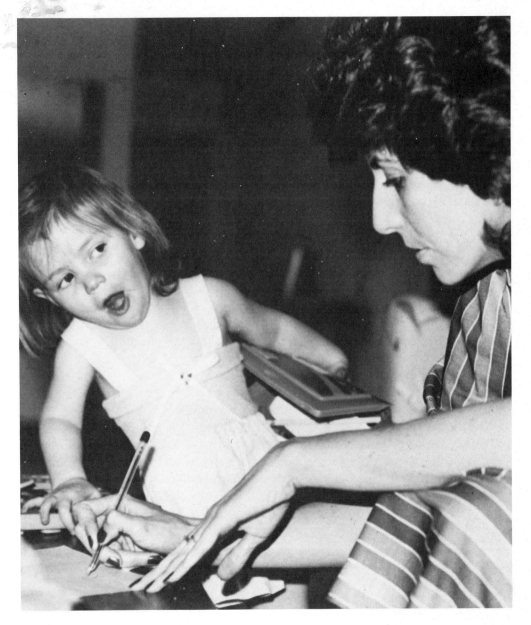

While the motor skills of two-year olds tend to develop at a steady rate, children's speaking skills often advance in sudden leaps. Due to these spurts in development, same-age peers may be in very different stages of language development.

"I'm doing the farm puzzle," Jeannette announced as she struggled to fit a puzzle piece into the wrong place. "This is a hard piece—this is a very hard piece."

"Me do it," Susan insisted, taking the piece out of Jeannette's hand and putting it in the puzzle.

"This is my puzzle," Jeannette replied. "You can have the zoo puzzle. You like the zoo puzzle better?"

"Me, me, me do," Susan insisted again, and within a few minutes she had helped Jeannette complete the puzzle.

Parents, overhearing this exchange between Jeannette and Susan,would be quick to note that Jeannette is by far the better talker. As Jeannette's parents, they might feel duly proud of their daughter's quickness. As Susan's parents, they might feel unnecessarily worried about their daughter's immature speech. However, it would be a mistake to conclude that Jeannette's precocious language development indicates greater intelligence. In fact, we do not know why some children, like Jeannette, are early talkers, but we do know that many of the differences between early and late talkers disappear by the time the children are three or four years old.

Whether a child is an early or late talker, significant growth takes place between two and three. Knowing more about the process of language development helps parents recognize and appreciate the progress their own child is making. In this chapter we will discuss three aspects of language development. First, we will look at how two year old children expand their ability to listen to language and to understand what it means. Second, we will explore the process of learning to speak, combining sounds to make words and then combining words to make sentences. Finally, we will focus on how children learn to converse with other people, how they use both their listening and speaking skills to communicate. Throughout the chapter we also suggest ways to enrich the language environment of two year old children. These ideas are not intended to speed up language development but to make it more enjoyable for both parents and children.

Learning to Listen

When children appear to be slow in acquiring speech, but are on target in every other way, parents need to rule out a hearing problem. Between one and three years of age, some children develop temporary hearing problems from the build-up of fluid in their ears. The condition can be identified in a routine pediatric check-up and is usually controlled by medication. In a small number of cases, tubes are inserted into the child's ears to allow for appropriate drainage.

A second consideration with the "slow to talk" child is the development of listening skills. If a child who is not speaking listens to language being spoken and follows simple directions, parents have a right to relax. Comprehension precedes production and, before long, their child will be talking. In the case of serious language delay, the child does not comprehend the meanning of words.

Listening Games

Parents who are concerned with encouraging language development can focus on listening games. One technique is to ask a series of "where" questions. Where questions, as opposed to what and why questions, can be answered nonverbally. For example, parents can pretend to lose or misplace something, and then invite a child to help with the search by asking questions out loud:

> "Now, where are my sandals? Come here, sandals." (Turning to child.) "Do you have my sandals on? Hmmm, no you don't. Well, where are they? . . . Oh, you found them in the closet."

Probably the best version of this game occurs when parents look for missing children. Then they have the opportunity to stimulate listening by proposing the most absurd ideas. Stacey had recently learned to open closet doors, so whenever things got unusually quiet around the house her parents were pretty sure she was hiding in some closet. The only question was— which one? "We better go find Stacey," her mother would announce in a loud voice. "Yes, let's try our bedroom first," answered Stacey's father in an equally loud voice. "Do you think she's in the jewelry box?" asked the mother. "Probably not," replied the father, "but she might be." "Hmm . . . not there," mused the mother. "Oh, no, I bet I threw her in the dirty clothes hamper by mistake this morning!" Long before her mother came up with this preposterous theory, Stacey's presence was made evident by her stifled giggles inside the closet. "Maybe I had better look in the closet before we go to the washing machine," Stacey's father offhandedly suggested . "Well, what do you know—here she is—in our closet."

Singing to a two-year old is another natural way to stimulate listening skills. Familiar songs can be elaborated by adding new verses. The general idea stays the same, which makes it easier for the child to understand, but each new verse creates a different image. "Old McDonald's Farm," for example, is a song of this type. Parents can keep thinking of new animals and new animal sounds for the farm. There is no reason, however, to stop with that. The farm can be populated with vehicles, machines, and anything else that makes a distinctive sound.

One day Steven's father started to sing, "The Bear Went Over the Mountain," mainly because he couldn't think of any other song to sing. Steven asked for more, so his father began to sing about transportation, a popular topic with Steven. "The bear drove a motorcycle, the bear drove a motorcycle, the bear drove a motorcycle, up to the top of the mountain." "More," said Steven. Soon the bear was driving all kinds of trucks and highway equipment. "Why just the bear?" thought Steven's father, who was getting a little bored. "The lion drove the school bus . . . The mouse drove a cement mixer . . . The giraffe came on roller skates." Steven's father was enjoying the unique traffic jam on top of the mountain.

Listening games like the ones we have described are invariably products of the moment. Parents discover them as if by chance, because they take the time to relax and let their minds take off. They instinctively know what subjects are especially important to their child, and they let their own imagination and the child's excited response be their guides.

Listening to Books

One of the most striking differences between the families we visited was their use of books. It was not uncommon for parents to tell us that they spent from two to four hours every day reading to their two-year old. Other parents spent virtually no time reading to their children. However, even among families where it was obvious that books were seldom used, the children showed an intense interest when we began to read to them. The desire of a two-year old to listen as an adult reads is an authentic phenomenon.

Toddlers like to name the objects in a picture book. Two-year olds continue to be interested in labeling pictures. Books especially designed for this purpose, like those by Richard Scary, are very popular. The children learn to recognize and to pronounce the names of exotic animals and specialized vehicles that they are not likely to see in the real world. In addition, there are numerous instances in which labeling within the simplified context of a book leads to recognition of real objects in the outside world.

Amy, for example, became interested in a book of signs. Her favorite sign was EXIT. To her parents' amazement, she began to point out EXIT signs in restaurants and stores. Then she started noticing STOP signs, IN and OUT signs, and ON signs. The sign book they read at home was clearly the inspiration for these discoveries.

The big leap in development occurs when children realize that there is a connection between the pages, that the pictures and words tell a story. This discovery seems to be a gradual one, like piecing together a puzzle. Each time a favorite book is read, a bit more of the story is recognized. Erik's favorite book at two years of age was a book about a birthday party. Having recently celebrated his own birthday, it was easier for him to follow the events in the story. Reading the book both refreshed his memory and provided an imaginary party. If every day could not be his birthday, at least he could read the birthday book.

When children are first learning to follow a story, they insist on hearing it over and over. Parents get tired of this repetition but, in a surprisingly short time, two-year olds become interested in a wide variety of story themes. Their powers of imagination develop to the point where they can enjoy stories about experiences they have never had, such as taking a trip in a rocket, digging for gold in the desert, or having a pet kangaroo.

Most children will have favorites, and whenever a story is connected to a special experience in their lives, that story may become a temporary obsession. Airplane trips may produce a burst of interest in airplane stories, feeding the animals on a farm can lead to a fascination with farm stories, a visit to the doctor often stimulates extra interest in stories about hospitals.

When parents get too bored by this constant repetition, they can try recording a story on a tape recorder. If two-year old children are already familiar with a book, they are capable of listening to the story on tape and turning the pages by themselves at the right moment.

Parents can also make reading more interesting for themselves by expanding a story. Although children do not like leaving out part of a story, they often welcome adding more to it. One way to embellish a story is to add dialogue. The pictures in most children's books include incidental characters, a squirrel in a tree, or a mouse behind a rock. These characters may not play a role in the story, but there is no reason why they cannot become involved. If "Curious George" crashes his bike, the squirrel who is looking on in the picture can say, "I hope George is all right," or "I wish I had a bike like that," or any number of other things. Once children grasp the idea that any character in a story can talk at any time, they can create additional dialogue. When reading the story of the tortoise and the hare, for example, Nicole added that the hare was sleeping because he went to bed late last night (after visiting his cousins) and that he felt sad to sleep alone.

Two year old children are especially interested in stories that address their fears and anxieties. At this age, children may become especially concerned about things being broken or lost, about people being injured or abandoned. It is no coincidence that the "Curious George" stories have been so popular for over thirty years. The two-year old can easily identify with a little monkey who is always making a mess, breaking important objects, getting lost, or investigating forbidden places.

Sometimes children become so involved in the imaginative experience of a story that they cannot accept one of these fearful occurrences. Kori really liked stories about a giant dog named Clifford. Clifford had a habit of rolling over and smashing things that got in his way. In one story he rolled on the family car and smashed it. Kori became quite upset and insisted, "Clifford no smash car. Clifford no smash car." The imaginative fear had become too real and Kori had to deny that it had happened. Kori's mother suggested that Clifford could fix the car. "No," replied Kori, "Clifford no have hands." Kori had become a strict realist as far as this event was concerned.

When children indicate an unwillingness to accept an imaginative experience that is too fearful, that part of the story can be skipped. Robert, like many children, was straightforward in his solution to this problem. If he did not like part of a story, he announced, "The End," and slammed the book shut. Because young children cannot read by themselves, it is important to give them some degree of control over the activity. If they want to skip an objectionable page, or stop the story in the middle, parents should be accommodating.

Listening to Television

Many two-year olds like to watch "Sesame Street" and they may have a few favorite cartoon shows, family shows, or other children's programs. Without a doubt they listen to the language on these programs, but our impression is that they concentrate on processing the visual information. Television is primarily a visual medium, and the pace of information is fast and full of special effects. Two year old children certainly recognize familiar faces, like Bert and Ernie. They may even recognize certain skits between the two Muppets. But the meaning of Bert and Ernie's conversation does not seem to sink in very far. The children do not ask many questions about what they hear and they do not imitate the language of the Muppets in their own speech or imaginative play.

Most two-year olds also are exposed to adult television programs. Invar-

iably they pay more attention to the advertisements than to the programs. The nature of the product being advertised seems to be irrelevant. They are just as interested in a commercial for aspirin as they are in a toy advertisement. There probably are several reasons why a young child is so attracted to commercials. They often include catchy music and animation. The close-ups of people staring straight into the camera create a personal atmosphere that may appeal to children. Yet the impression remains that two-year olds are drawn to commercials because of the language. They seem to be listening to the words, even though many of them are too hard to understand. Whenever the commercial is shown, the same words are heard, each one following the other in a completely predictable pattern. For this reason, commercials represent a chance for two-year olds to practice their listening skills. It is a challenge to anticipate and then confirm the sequence of words.

When children indicate that they are learning to recognize television commercials, it is a sign that they are ready to listen to simple story tapes. Tapes consisting of stories no longer than a few minutes are available. These tapes have the same appeal as commercials—clearly articulated language, a musical background, and a short message that can be repeated over and over. The listening stimulation they provide, however, is much more meaningful to two-year olds than that of television commercials.

Whether children are listening to a story tape or an appropriate television program, this kind of listening activity is less flexible and less personal than other activities we have discussed. Singing a song, reading a book, or playing a listening game involves personal interaction between parents and children. These activities are adapted to fit individual interests and styles. They are open-ended rather than fixed, alive rather than canned. The performance on a television program may be much more polished and entertaining, but two-year olds generally prefer to listen to a real person who knows them. Sitting on a lap and reading a book is better than watching the best that show business can offer.

Of course, real people are not always available to talk to a two-year old and, in these situations, it is reasonable to substitute electronically produced language. But even when children are encouraged to sit in front of a television set or record player, the experience will be more productive if parents participate to some degree. Perhaps they can talk occasionally with the children about what is happening; perhaps they can note the topics that most intrigue their children and bring them up in future conversations. Television and other electronic media represent an ever-present source of stimulation and, when used sparingly, add variety and spice to the language environment of two-year olds. However, when used so often that they replace listening activities with real people, these technological marvels actually impoverish the language environment of young children.

Learning to Speak

Learning to listen may be basic to language development, but learning to speak is more significant to parents. We eagerly anticipate a child's first words and, when they appear, we start listening for the child's first sentences. There often is a relatively long time, six months or more, during which a child's speaking ability seems to expand slowly. This dormant period typically occurs between one and two years of age. When it happens, parents become worried: "Debbie understands almost everything we say, and she can pronounce words—why doesn't she talk more?" Then one day Debbie's parents realize that her vocabulary is bursting with new words. Now she only needs to hear a word once before it is picked up.

This pattern of slow, almost non-existent vocabulary growth, followed by a rapid spurt, is not the only way children learn to speak, but it is common. One reason seems to be that, during the period of slow growth, children are learning how to control different speech sounds. Once they have mastered enough sounds to repeat many of the words they hear, their speaking vocabulary suddenly expands.

We take for granted this ability to imitate speech, but in reality it is a small miracle. Without observing the tongue and palate movements that are necessary to produce each consonant and vowel, we somehow learn to make these sounds and to coordinate them into words. A word like "helicopter," for example, requires a complicated sequence of speech acts. No wonder a child just starting to speak may say "heh" or "caw" or mumble something unintelligible.

If a two year old child's understanding of language is progressing satisfactorily, and yet the child is slow to speak, there is a good possibility that it is due to articulation problems. Usually children solve these articulation problems by themselves in a few months and rapidly catch up in speaking skills. We do not know why some young children master the basic rules of articulation more quickly than others, although we do know that children who are poor chewers or children who do a lot of drooling are likely to have articulation problems. In any event, articulation skills are not fully developed for many years. A two-year old who understands language but does not articulate clearly is not a candidate for speech therapy.

The best way to encourage two-year olds to improve their articulation is to give them opportunities to talk to a wide range of people. Gillian used to talk on the telephone to her father at the office every day. Other people in the office also wanted to say "hello." Gillian usually called right after lunch and she often reported on the food she did not like. "I no like cely," she announced one day. "You don't like jelly?" the secretary asked. "No, no," said

Gillian, "I no like cely." "I don't understand you, Gillian," answered the secretary. "Soup," Gillian explained. Although the secretary never did figure out that Gillian meant celery soup, our example illustrates the process by which misunderstanding creates pressure for better articulation.

The Transition From Inflection to Words

Talking is a matter of inflection as well as words. Inflection is the music of speech, the pitch and tone of voice, and the rhythm of phrases. Babies are more attentive to inflection than to words. When spoken in a horrified tone of voice, a word like "hot" communicates a sense of danger to babies long before they understand the specific meaning of the word. Between the ages of one and two, many children demonstrate an amazing control of inflection. They chatter away in familiar inflection patterns, and their language sounds real to us, even though we cannot identify the words.

Toddlers use their control of inflection to communicate. They send inflectional messages – "I'm happy, I'm angry, I want more food, I want out of my crib, I want to be carried." Using words to communicate represents a new strategy, and some children seem unwilling to give up the old style that parents already understand.

April had mastered every detail of the daily schedule in her family and she was clever at getting what she wanted. If she wanted to hear a story, she would hand a book to her mother, make an excited, pleading sound, and then clap her hands. April's mother knew the routine was manipulative but it was so cute. April's father, on the other hand, responded well when April stamped her little foot and made a menacing sound with her voice. He found this "fierce" behavior quite charming.

April was only twenty-four months old and her parents were not concerned about the fact that she used few words. In the future, however, they are likely to find her inflectional messages less appealing. They will expect April to change her strategy for communicating, to use words primarily and inflection secondarily.

Parents in this kind of situation may subscribe to the "lazy tongue" theory. Essentially this theory is as follows: If children understand language and they can pronounce a few words clearly, the reason they do not talk more is that they are lazy. They will not make the effort to say a word when a grunt, a squeal, or a gesture will work instead. According to this theory, the solution to the problem lies in making sure that laziness is not rewarded. Parents are advised to stop responding to a child's inflectional messages. If the child wants a drink of milk, make him say the word "milk" before you give it to him. Stop coddling the child, and force him to use language.

From our perspective, learning to talk is an extremely complex and difficult task. If some children are slow to speak, it is simplistic to assume that it is caused by laziness. Moreover, we doubt very much the efficacy of forcing children to communicate. Imagine yourself in a foreign language class, twenty-four hours per day, where you could not watch your favorite television program, eat your favorite desserts, read your favorite magazines, or call your favorite friends until you could pronounce certain words in the foreign language. Given the circumstances, you might very well learn these words, but what would your attitude be toward the instructor? Would you feel like communicating with him? Those who survived and succeeded in such a foreign language class would feel justifiably proud of their accomplishment, but there also would be numerous dropouts. We suspect the same kind of process happens with young children. Forcing children to talk will cause many to withdraw even more.

One of the ways to recognize the ingredients of a facilitative environment is to look at the families in which children talk early. Typically we find parents who are very sensitive to their child's tone of voice and mood. These parents respond to any messages their children send, whether they are based on words, inflection, or gesture.

Jennifer, at one-year old, had developed a pointing game. As soon as her mother picked her up, she pointed to a window or picture across the room.

She expected her mother to go over there and talk about what she was seeing.

Mother:	"Look, Jennifer, there's a bird out in the tree. Isn't she a pretty bird?"
Jennifer:	"Da, da."
Mother:	"That's right, there is some dirt on the window."
Jennifer:	"Da, da."
Mother:	"Oh, you want down? O.K."
Jennifer:	"Da, da."
Mother:	"Oh, I see what you got – your duck."
Jennifer:	"Da, da."
Mother:	"Yes, the duck is like the bird in the tree. Very good."

Jennifer's mother discovered a multitude of messages in Jennifer's "Da, da." Perhaps some of these messages were not even there – it does not really matter. The important thing is her mother's orientation. She assumes that the more she responds to Jennifer's messages, no matter how ill-formed, the more messages Jennifer will send. In our experience, this is exactly what happens. Jennifer's mother usually responds with some verbalization. Even when she is granting a request, such as putting Jennifer down, she describes the action. By modeling a variety of messages, she undoubtedly helps Jennifer to formulate her own.

Jennifer is still using inflections and gestures as her primary means of communication. At some point she will need to abandon this strategy in favor of words. In Jennifer's case, we can predict this transfer will be accomplished easily, so easily in fact that her parents may never notice it. Jennifer will find the transition simple because she has so many different messages to send. She will not be satisfied much longer to point in the general direction she wants her mother to go. She will start pointing at specific objects, wanting to hold them and wanting her mother to talk about them. Pointing to the cupboard when she is hungry will be even less satisfactory. She may get a cracker when she wants the honey. As the specificity of her messages increases, so will her incentive to use words.

We do not want to imply that when children are slow to talk it necessarily means their parents are unresponsive. There are a number of possible reasons for delayed speech. Our point is that trying to force children to talk is not a particularly effective way to develop language. We recommend trying to expand the number of messages children want to send. Parents can encourage more messages by pointing out interesting sights, by describing their children's actions, by playing listening games, and by reading books. We believe that, if children want to communicate a variety of messages, they will eventually find that words are necessary.

Combining Words Into Sentences

Once children begin to use a large variety of one-word messages, it is only a matter of a few weeks or months before the words are combined into sentences. Some children go through a stage of two-word sentences, followed by three and then four-word sentences, systematically building their grammatical expertise. Other children use familiar phrases and simple sentence frames from the start. The progression from one to several words is impressive enough, but the grammatical elaboration that soon follows is truly astounding. After six months to a year of talking in sentences, children have acquired the basic grammar of English.

This feat is accomplished without any direct instruction from adults. Children listen to the language around them and come up with their own rules of grammar. Imitation plays a part in that children pick up the phrases and vocabulary of their parents, but all children have their own systems for creating sentences.

We know young children have their own rules of grammar because they systematically make mistakes they have never heard. For example, a two-year old may say, "Me going store." The children have never heard anyone else use "me" like this. However, they have learned from listening that "me" is used as a self-reference, and therefore they use it in all cases. We might say they have learned only part of the rule in standard English.

The grammar of children is sometimes more logical than the grammar of their parents because the children have not learned that every rule has exceptions. For example, when children learn to form plurals by adding an "s," they change foot to foots or feets. When they learn to form the past tense by adding "ed," they change go to goed, or hit to hitted.

Between the ages of two and three, children learn to fill in the little words that are missing in their earlier sentences. "Me going Mama store," becomes "I am going with my Mama to the store." Words like "the, with, my, to" are not usually necessary to understand simple sentences, but they specify the meaning more precisely. One day parents suddenly realize that their children are routinely inserting common prepositions and adjectives into sentences.

There are two kinds of sentences that are particularly difficult to construct, although both are common. These sentences are questions and negative statements. Their combination, a negative question, is even harder. Parents can watch their two-year olds progressing step by step with these sentences. One of the first steps in forming questions is to learn special question words that can be placed at the beginning of a sentence: "Why you fixing my tricycle?" "Where we going?" A second step, which often does not begin to appear until the age of three, is to use the correct helping verb at the beginning of the question: "Why *are* you fixing my tricycle?" "Where *are* we going?" The development of negative sentences is somewhat similar. At

first children learn to add a negative word to the sentence: "I no like dogs." "I not going home." Later they begin to add the appropriate helping verb: "I *am* not going home." "I *do* not like dogs."

We have greatly simplified the complexities of questions and negative sentences. Most two-year olds have only begun the process of learning these rules. Several more years of listening and talking will be needed before they are fully understood. The best way to help children develop grammatical competence is to expose them to many examples of proper grammar and to encourage them to express themselves as much as possible. As we emphasized with articulation, it is conversation and not instruction that is the key to language development.

Two year old children also practice their grammar by talking to themselves. Typically, these monologues occur when children are quietly occupied, going to sleep, playing in the bathtub, or riding in a car. A child may start with a simple phrase and build it up into a more complex one: "Bye-bye, Nana. Have a nice time working on papers, Nana." The reverse exercise may occur, breaking a long phrase down into a simple one. Sometimes children invent substitute exercises: "Riding on a camel, riding on a boat, riding on a plane," or they practice making negative statements, "The car's too hot—not too hot; it's too far—not too far." Other drills may involve pronouns, pluralization, or any other grammatical rules children incorporate into their language at this age. The desire of children to master the rules of grammar is an amazing phenomenon.

Learning to Converse

Billy: "I want ketchup."

Mother: "Don't you remember, you broke it yesterday?"

Billy: "We buy more ketchup at store?"

Mother: "Sure, next time we go. How about mustard for your sandwich?"

Billy: "This mustard bites my mouth."

Mother: "Here, let's mix it with some mayonnaise."

Billy: "I don't like mayonnaise."

Mother: "Sure you do. You always eat it with salami."

Billy: "This is not salami. It's olive loaf."

Mother: "Well, it's the same thing really. Anyway, this isn't mayonnaise—it's mustardaise."

Billy: "Yea, mustardaise, we don't have no catsupaise—just mustardaise."

Mother: "And it will make your ears grow."

A conversation is both an exchange of information and a social interaction. Within the back and forth rhythm, we can see that Billy has developed considerable conversational skill. He can form questions, arguments, comments, and even a joke. As in many conversations with two-year olds, Billy's primary purpose in this exchange is to get adult help. He wants some improvement in his sandwich, and he uses language to affect his mother's behavior. Although the conversation does not focus on new information, several ideas are communicated. Catsup comes from stores, mayonnaise cuts the strong taste of mustard, and olive loaf is like salami. There also is a playful aspect to this conversation. Billy argues only half-heartedly about the mayonnaise and, when his mother invents a new term, he plays with it and comes up with his own new word. Using language to affect another person's behavior, to communicate ideas, and just for fun are the three aspects of conversation we will discuss in more detail.

Affecting Another Person's Behavior

At an early age, children begin to use language to make their wishes known. Between the ages of two and three, they learn to back up these requests with arguments. The "no" of the toddler gives way to more sophisticated forms of self-assertion. As Kori put it when she was told to go inside, "I am Myla Kori Bardige, and I'm not going inside." Loosely translated, this argument seems to be: "I am an important person and, therefore, when I say 'no,' it carries weight."

There is a strong imitative element in these early arguments. Kori's mother used Kori's full name when she meant business, and Kori was imitating this practice. Such imitative language is usually easy to tolerate because it is so entertaining. Brad informed his mother, "You drive me up a wall," when he was told to take a nap; and Erik snorted, "fridiculous," when told to put on his coat before going outside.

Two-year olds go beyond using imitative language to contradict their parents. They also turn parents' arguments back on them. Lisa liked to answer the phone, and she resisted giving the phone to her mother by saying, "You don't know them." Randy refused to eat his dinner because, "I'm a baby and babies don't have to eat dinner." Matthew told his father, "You have to share your tools with me 'cause I share my tools with you."

When children use the phrases and arguments of their parents, they may not successfully control their parents' behavior, but at least some of the tension surrounding the conversation is released. Sometimes parents laugh and agree with the child's point of view; sometimes they insist on their own perspective, but in a gentler tone of voice. Although the arguments of two year old children often make us smile, we should remember that they are serious. Children do not argue with us in order to be amusing, but in order to make a point. Sooner or later they will push their arguments far enough to annoy us or even to make us angry.

It was funny the first time Patty said she was "too busy" to put on her clothes. After being late to nursery school every day for two weeks, however, the situation was different. Stephanie's mother smiled when Stephanie said she was "not perky" and needed another vitamin pill. But Stephanie could not be convinced that one was enough and she turned breakfast into a tense time by continually whining, "I need more."

Probably the most difficult kind of argument to handle is being told to be quiet. Jon told his parents to stop reminding him about the toilet by saying, "I want done that." Other children are even more direct. They cut parents off in the middle of their lectures by saying, "No talk" or "Go away." These responses are infuriating to parents who are already inflamed.

On the one hand, it is unrealistic to anticipate laughing off every argument that a two-year old formulates. On the other hand, it does not make much sense to go to the other extreme and always punish a two-year old for arguing, or "talking back." The most primitive and least flexible way to exercise control in a conversation is to force the conversation to end, and this is what we do when we do not allow children to argue with us. The ability of two year old children to argue follows naturally from their growing conversational skill. If we refuse to let children argue with us, we are encouraging them to drop out of future conversations by ignoring us. They may appear to be more polite, but what they are really doing is paying less attention to us.

Many arguments with two year old children cannot be resolved satisfactorily because the children do not understand the concepts involved in the argument. For example, when Terry's parents told him that he needed to go to bed in order to rest, he insisted that he was not tired. Indeed, his energy level was very high because he speeded up when he got tired. Telling Terry that he needed rest because he would be very busy after his nap was no good either. He could not understand the relationship between rest and energy, and his ability to project himself into the future was quite imprecise.

Terry's parents realized that he did not understand their explanations, but they still allowed Terry to argue with them. They accepted Terry's feelings that this issue was an important topic for conversation.

The more young children argue, the better they become at it and the more likely they are to gain a compromise. At some point every parent reaches a limit and refuses to argue about a subject any more. But until that point is reached, two year old children are learning about a valuable aspect of conversation, the fine art of negotiation and compromise.

When compromise is not possible, children may opt for saving face. One day Stacy did not like what the family was having for dinner. "I want a hot dog," she told her mother. "I'm sorry, we don't have any," was the reply. Stacy consoled herself by saying, "Maybe tomorrow." Her mother doubted that hot dogs would be served the next day, but she let the comment pass, knowing that by tomorrow Stacy would have forgotten about it. Beverly's attempt to save face was even more transparent. She was denied dessert because she had not eaten her dinner, and as the rest of the family ate their ice cream, she rationalized, "I don't like ice cream anyway." Having the last word is a Pyrrhic victory, but it often is sufficient for two year old children. Not able to control the situation, they can at least control the conversation.

Communicating Ideas

The most typical thoughts two year old children try to communicate are descriptions of what they see. Evan, who was just two, pointed out every McDonald's that the family passed. Lisa, at two and one half, concentrated on finding Pizza Huts. Laura, a three-year old, noticed McDonald's, Burger King, Pizza Hut, International Pancake House, Kentucky Fried Chicken, and Denny's.

Whether it is restaurants, trucks, animals, or any other category of objects that is especially interesting to two year old children, we see a similar pattern. Children start with a particular favorite and look for it everywhere in their environment. The idea they are communicating is, "There is another one of those interesting things called . . ." After days or weeks of exhaustive searching, they often switch to a new favorite. Gradually the category expands and the observational skills of the children become more flexible. They watch for, and comment on, a variety of favorites.

Stating the name of an object represents a minimal description. Between two and three, children learn to describe what they see in more detail. Negative characteristics are frequently prominent in these descriptions. Things are "messy," "greasy," "dirty," "stinky," "broken," "slippery," "lost," "tricky." However, children at this age are also interested in talking about more objective attributes of objects, such as color and size.

Brian said "red" whenever the family stopped at a traffic light, and then he yelled "green" as soon as the light changed. Stacy learned the color orange by looking for Union 76 signs. Colors, like other categories, are seldom learned all at once. Children start with one or two favorite colors, then switch to other favorites, and after a year or more of trial and error, the whole spectrum has been distinguished.

Size terms form a different pattern. They come in opposites. Kathy received a little chair on her second birthday. For several months she always brought the chair into the living room when visitors came and compared her "little" chair to her father's "big" chair. "Big" and "little" (or "tiny") stand out for almost all two-year olds. However, many other opposite terms are common also—tall-short, good-bad, easy-hard, first-last, slow-fast, up-down, in-out, hot-cold, loud-quiet, pretty-ugly. The precise terms that children learn depend on the language they hear and the objects that interest them.

Children often learn one term first in a pair of opposites. Andy learned "loud" before "quiet" because large trucks on the highway frightened him when they passed the car. However, Erik learned "quiet" first because his mother urged him to "Be quiet and take a nap." Eventually, both terms in a pair of opposites are learned and then, as with Kathy and the chairs, children tend to juxtapose opposites in the same conversation. "This is slow," said Jeffrey, pushing his toy cement truck. By way of contrast, he picked up a race car and said, "This is fast." Then he skimmed the race car across the floor and watched it bounce off a wall.

Opposite games may evolve. Patti and her father played a game with a large cardboard box. Patti's father dropped picture playing cards through a slot while Patti, who was inside the box, pushed the cards back out. "In goes a bear . . . out comes a skunk." "In goes a duck . . . out comes an elephant." Sitting in his highchair, Erik looked at his legs and stretched them out in front of him. "Now I'm tall." Tucking his legs back under the chair, he said, "Now I'm short."

In describing the world around them, there are two little words that many young children find especially useful:"too" and "like." Toys are "too high" to reach; puzzles are "too hard;" clothes are "too big" or "too small;" there are "too may bugs" or there is "too much snow." "Too" is an ideal word for expressing feelings of frustration over an excess in the state of things. "Like," which is another very flexible term, is ideal for talking about similarities. A pickle can look "like an alligator," the moon can look "like a banana," a football game on television can look "like Wheaties." When "too" and "like" appear in the descriptions children use, a new level of subtlety is possible. It is interesting for parents to observe the kind of excesses and similarities on which their children comment.

Probably the most fascinating thing about the descriptive statements of young children is the ability to use words in new ways. Robert did not have a word to convey his dislike of cherries and grapes in fruit cocktail, so he referred to them as "dirty." They were a kind of dirt in his dessert. Erik did not have a word to describe the jumble of toys he had created on the floor, so he called it "a big traffic jam." Kristin called her mother's bra "a white nipple." Raymond told the doctor that he didn't want a "bleeding." This kind of word creativity gives us another indication of the contrasts and analogies that children see around them.

In many conversations that focus on the communication of ideas, two year old children take the role of asking questions. Although questions may be used to tease parents or simply to extend a conversation, two-year olds also use questions to solicit information. "What's that?" may be a genuine question when a child sees an unusual object and wants to know its name. Another early question is "where?" and some very interesting "where" questions may appear as children become more aware of disappearing objects. Mark asked where a balloon was after it had popped. Clarence asked where Big Bird went after the television had lost its picture. Matthew asked where the soapsuds went as they dribbled down the drain.

"Why" questions are a new development between two and three, and it often takes a while for children to grasp the meaning of "why." Once they learn to use this question form appropriately, they tend to ask about the purpose or intention behind events. "Why you spank the cat?" "Why you painting house?"

Accidents are particularly hard to explain. Kelly asked her mother several times a day for a week, "Why Daddy drop peanut butter?" With less patience each time, her mother explained that it had been an accident, the peanut butter had slipped, Daddy wasn't using both hands. Kelly found these explanations unsatisfactory because they did not specify an intention or a purpose. Breaking the peanut butter jar was not an intentional act and neither did it serve any purpose. So Kelly remained confused as to why it had happened and she kept asking for clarification.

Another new question form between the ages of two and three is "Who?" Children discover that every person has a name. Naturally they expect their parents to know these names, just as they know the names of objects. A child may ask for the name of the mailman or the trash collector, the clerks in the stores, other passengers in an elevator, or even for the names of people driving by in cars.

Although two-year olds usually do not ask many "When" questions, they use other questions to find out about time sequences: "What we do after nap?" "We go swimming today?" " 'Sesame Street' on T.V.?" After numerous conversations of this kind, the children may pick up a standard form for expressing simple temporal relationships: "After I take a nap, then we go to restaurant?" or "First we go to Grandma's house, then we go shopping?"

The ability of young children to express sequential information is limited, but they do show a great desire to talk about the past. Parents find themselves describing the events of the day to their two-year olds as they go to sleep at night. This routine starts innocently enough, for it is natural to remind children of a pleasant experience before they drift off to sleep. However, the intense interest of many children in these reminiscences leads to more and more detailed conversation.

Extended conversation about any topic leads away from the immediate time and place. Having just begun to communicate in sentences, two-year olds are eager to explore this transcendent quality of language. Their capacity to appreciate remote times and places may be somewhat limited. The place they describe may be the neighborhood drug store and the time may be earlier that day. Their memory may seem rigid, almost mechanical, to us. Every time Halloween was mentioned, Jeffrey said, "Remember the spider?" referring to an impressive Halloween display he had seen at the grocery store. Yet he continued to listen intently to his mother's recollection of putting on his costume, 'trick or treating,' etc.

Some parents instinctively relate present experiences to similar ones in the past. "Remember" is among their favorite words. Other parents do not talk to two-year olds in this way. It is our impression that nearly all two year old children welcome this kind of conversation. The recent past holds the same fascination as a story book for, in reality, each child's daily activities make up his own life story.

The parent's role is just as important in other conversations involving the communication of ideas. The questions of two year old children are often poorly formed, and close listening is required to find out what the children are really curious about. It also takes considerable time and effort to answer the questions in a way that young children can understand. Descriptive comparisons and analogies by two-year olds are usually brief, and parents need to expand them in order to sustain the conversation. The children are interested in talking about what they see, but their verbal ability lags behind their ability to observe similarities and differences. Whether a converation consists primarily of descriptive comments, a question and answer exchange, or a reminiscence of a past experience, it is up to parents to keep the ideas flowing back and forth.

Conversational Play and Humor

One of the functions of language at every age is play. The toddler who babbles happily as he removes books from the bookcase is bubbling over with good cheer. He is not trying to control or communicate, just to celebrate his mood with some verbal music. More and more of this music is set to words as the language of children matures. The two-year old who is dunking her doll in the bathtub repeats to herself in a sing-song chant, "in and out—in and out." Almost every monologue has elements of playful poetry, even if its primary purpose is to guide or clarify the child's activity. As Lynn drew a picture, she murmured, "Where did my chalk go? I am making a nice circle here. Where's the sponge, hon? Here's the sponge, hon."

The appearance of verbal humor is also a new development between the ages of two and three. As children come to understand the sense of language, they see the humor of nonsense. Nouns predominate in the early language of children and therefore noun nonsense predominates in early humor.

Michael gave his mother a double-take the first time she asked him if he wanted some more "blibber." She had a dish of noodles in her hand: "Was this some kind of trick?" he wondered. "Do you want some more blibber?—

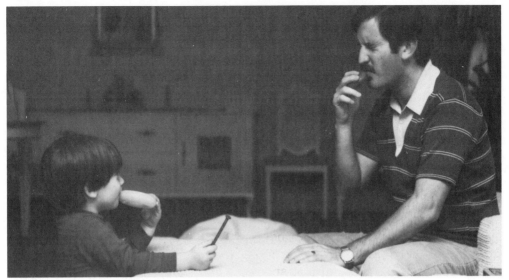

or is it blubber?" "No," roared Michael, "just noodles," and he grabbed the dish. The broad smile on his face showed that he had understood the joke and was waiting for more of this crazy talk.

Noun nonsense evolves naturally from nursery rhymes that children have memorized. "Mary had a little elephant," recited Chad's mother, as Chad giggled. Robert, who didn't like sad endings anyway, was much happier when the last little piggy went to the Pizza Hut instead of home.

Another natural opportunity to introduce humor arises when two year old children start the game of "what's this?" After dinner every night Brad insisted that his father sit down and look at a Richard Scary book with him. "What's this?" Brad asked, pointing to a picture of a fried egg. "Why, that's a fried floozle," said his father. "No, silly, that's an egg."

Of course, the unparalleled master of noun nonsense is Dr. Seuss. Most of his stories are too complicated for two year old children to follow, but they enjoy listening to the word concoctions. A particular phrase may get singled out and become part of a daily game. For example, Andy liked the phrase "a wocket in your pocket," so his parents amused him with similar questions, "Is there a wup in your cup?" "Is there a wub in the tub?"

Two year old children are also beginning to enjoy the humor of mispronunciation. Chad quickly picked up his parents' nighttime routine of asking, "Are you thoisty?" In Sherri's family, everyone gets a "hugarooni," which sounds a lot more special than the normal hug. Families make up strange and humorous pet names for each other, such as "Weenie Brandini" for the more pedestrian "Brandi," or "Jody Pody" and "Sherry Cherrie."

In describing the humor that parents and two year old children share, we do not mean to suggest that there is a constant atmosphere of hilarity. Humor provides the accent to conversation, the spice. A steady diet of it soon becomes tedious for everyone. Moreover, a sense of verbal humor is just beginning to develop in children between the ages of two and three. Adults take the lead in introducing funny ideas. During the next few years, the children's attempts to be funny will increase greatly as they learn to participate in the give-and-take of verbal humor.

Usually there is an element of teasing in verbal humor and the distinction between being playful versus being cruel can become blurred. A child may feel belittled, rather than amused, by adult antics. More common at this age, however, is a feeling of confusion. As Michelle put it when her mother used nonsense words, "Talk nice."

On the other hand, parents may become upset with the over-exuberant silliness of children, especially if it is interpreted as show-off behavior. When we visited Janet, she wanted to read a book. The story consisted of animals talking about themselves. On one page, the bee said, "God helps me make honey." Janet teased her father by saying "Me?", knowing full well that it was not she who made honey. This routine was repeated on every page, and when it did not sufficiently amuse her father or us, Janet began to pretend to eat the pictures, saying things like, "I'm eating grass." In this case, neither Janet's father nor we were upset with Janet's determined effort to assume the center of the stage, for this was the purpose of our visit. However, on another occasion her humor might have been less welcome.

*   *   *

Language development between the ages of two and three brings out the teacher in most parents. It is a subject they feel confident teaching, having been successful speakers for many years, and the rapid growth in the language of children demonstrates that their pupils are eager and intelligent. Very often the teacher-parent trains the pupil-child to do some language tricks. Teacher: "What does Ronald McDonald say?" Pupil: "We do it all for you...oou." Most parents sense that these tricks are peripheral to the mainstream of language development. They are the frosting on the cake.

Occasionally, however, the tricks assume more importance than they deserve. Parents become overly concerned about teaching children to speak courteously, or to pronounce words properly, or to read flash cards. In one family where we felt such a pattern existed, the mother proudly asked her two and a half year old daughter to recite her full name, address and telephone number. The little girl dutifully rattled off a reasonable approximation of the correct words, but obviously with little comprehension of their meaning. In itself there is nothing wrong with teaching a young child her address and telephone number, even if she does not understand what she is

talking about. What is disturbing is the narrow view of language development that may lie behind this practice. As we have mentioned several times throughout this chapter, language is a live and spontaneous process in which parents and children can express their feelings to each other and explore the world together. It is not a bag of tricks handed down from one generation to the next.

Many parents do a splendid job of stimulating their two-year old's language. They converse freely with their children, answering both questions and complaints. They read many books with their children in a way that is both informative and entertaining. However, even these parents could often benefit from loosening up their role as language teachers.

One conscientious mother we visited had been playing with her son in a pretend situation before we arrived. He was pretending that a set of plastic rings were various fish. "Find me the biggest fish," the mother requested. "No, that's not the biggest fish," the mother continued. "The biggest one is right behind you. How many fish am I holding in my hand now?" Although this mother was taking advantage of an imaginative play situation to extend her child's vocabulary, she was missing the real fun of conversation. Fortunately, later in the day this same mother resumed the fish game with her son. This time she was not playing teacher, and both mother and son had more fun.

Mother: "Thank you for finding me the little fish. I will hide him under the rock so the big fish will not scare him."

Child: "Big fish scaring him. Big fish swimming-swimming-swimming."

Mother: "Be careful, big fish—you may get stuck under the rock."

Child: "Big fish swimming under the rock. Be careful swimming under the rock."

Chapter 5
IMAGINATIVE PLAY

"Picnic's ready, everybody sit down. No, Big Bird, you sit up over here and don't fall down." As we watch Melinda, who is two and a half, arranging her "Sesame Street" characters around the picnic table, we get the feeling that we have just walked into the middle of an elaborate stage production. Melinda is a rather bossy director instructing the various characters as to how they should play their parts.

> "Want a hamburger, Big Bird?" Melinda asks as she shoves a red poker chip into Big Bird's beak. "Yes, I want a hamburger," Big Bird answers in a high squeaky voice. "So do I," answers Melinda as she pours some imaginary ketchup onto a stack of poker chips.

Although adults may do their own kind of pretending, "pretend play" is the special trademark of childhood. Whether the youngster is surrounded by a roomful of Fisher Price miniatures, or out in a backyard with nothing but a clothespin, the child's imagination creates its special alchemy. The Fisher Price characters walk and talk and the old-fashioned clothespin becomes a soldier, an airplane, or a fishing rod. In this chapter we will look at imaginative play from several points of view:

What are the major developmental advances in imaginative play between the ages of two and three? How can we describe individual differences in imaginative play behavior? What purpose does imaginative play serve? How can we foster imaginative play?

Developmental Advances

Two year old children are in a transition period for the development of imaginative play. One year old toddlers are more apt to be imitators than pretenders. As they jabber into a toy telephone or sweep the floor with an oversized broom, they are copying, as accurately as they can, a performance they have witnessed. But as children approach two years, subtle changes can be seen in their style of playing. Imaginary play episodes and themes begin to emerge. Let's take a closer look at these developmental changes.

As young as two years old, when she had just about mastered the two-word phrase, Kori's favorite play theme was a trip to Star Market. At first the trip consisted of slinging a purse across her shoulder, mounting her rocking horse, and chanting, "Star Market." A few months later, a new element was added

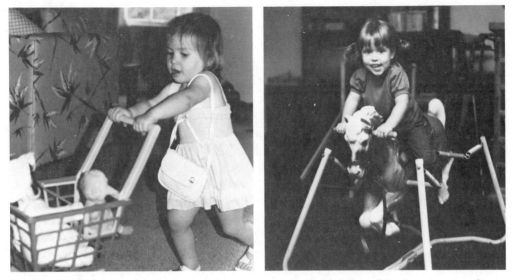

to the Star Market excursions. Kori recognized that Star Market was a place to buy things. Before mounting the rocking horse, she gathered up a paper bag and her favorite Raggedy Ann. "Go Star Market," she told Raggedy Ann. "Me buy peanut butter, orange juice, cherries."

Within the next six months, Kori's language took a quantum leap and the trips to Star Market became much more complicated. "Need a pencil and note pad, going to Star Market. You running out of peanut butter? You need margarine and paper towels?" Kori squiggled some lines on her notebook, gathered up Raggedy Ann, her mother's purse, a paper bag, and a set of keys. Struggling to carry everything in her arms, and seating herself on the top of a cardboard carton, she scooted along the floor. (The carton had replaced the rocking horse as her preferred mode of transportation.) "Vroom, vroom, vroom-going to Star Market - Mommy running out of peanut butter - Mommy running out of paper towels."

As we compare Kori's three renditions of the Star Market excursion, we see changes taking place in the way Kori uses imitation. In the first version, the imitative component is predominant. Kori slings the pocketbook over her shoulder exactly like her mother. As the trips become more elaborate, Kori is no longer limited to simply mimicking her mother's actions. Now she can act out a routine that expresses her own notion of what going to Star Market means: Star Market is where you buy important things that are good to eat or good for wiping up spills.

A young child is apt to be confused by a trip to the supermarket, to see it as a sequence of unconnected experiences: a hurried exit from the house, a drive in the car, a place with lots of noise and people, a cart with cans and boxes thrown in, a lady who rings a machine. As children return time and time again to the store, they begin to make sense out of these random impressions. Ultimately, they realize that running out of food, driving to the store, putting food in the basket, giving the cashier money, and bringing the food home are all part of the same event. Each time children play out a new pretend sequence, they demonstrate this emerging ability to recreate a sequence and to make sense out of a complex occurrence.

The repertoire of these play themes expands between the ages of two and three. Young two-year olds play mainly at eating, sleeping, driving, and cleaning up while older two-year olds include such activities in larger schemes. They go to the laundromat, the bank, the circus, or the zoo. They fish, camp out, go to church or to McDonald's. They may be gas station attendants, garbage collectors, taxi drivers, mailmen, doctors, or sales clerks. The increase in the number of play themes is related to the child's expanding life experiences. As children go to more places, see more people and do more things, they have an increasing variety of material to draw upon. The addition of new play themes also reflects a greater ability to organize and interpret new experiences.

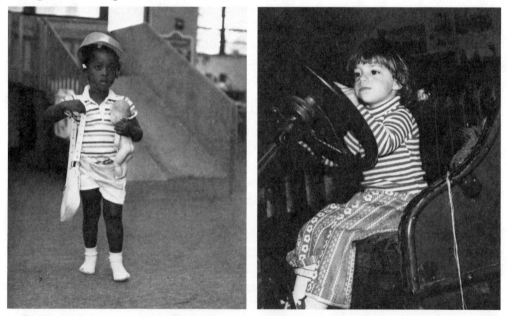

A final change in imaginative play within the third year is an increase in the role of language. As children gain more understanding of language, they respond more readily to the suggestions of adults. At the same time, their greater ability to use language enables them to direct the action, furnish the dialogue and supply the running commentary in a pretend production. The more adept the child is at using language, the more elaborate a production can become.

Andrew: "Here comes the big truck. Watch out everybody, big truck coming."

Father: "Sorry, big truck, you have to slow down. You are coming to the toll gate. Here's your ticket, Mr. Truck Driver."

Andrew: "Thank you, Mr. Man. Zoom...zoom, going up the mountain. Oops, flat tire."

Father: "Humm...that flat tire looks pretty serious. We'd better find the jack and jack up your truck."

Andrew: "Here's the jack. Fix the tire."

Father: "Let's hurry. Looks as if you've got ice cream in your truck. We don't want it to melt."

Andrew: "Yeh - got lots of ice cream and chocolate ice cream, strawberry and more ice cream."

Father: "You're making me hungry. How about giving me an ice cream sandwich while we repair this flat tire."

Individual Differences

In each home we visited, we encouraged the family to describe or demonstrate their favorite pretend themes. We found that two-year olds not only have favorite themes but have also developed a preferred style of pretending. In some of the families, the dominant method of pretending was role play—adopting the role of someone else or playing out an imaginary experience. In other families, the major way of pretending was through the creation of an imaginary world by animating toys, or by producing a story

line. We have labeled the first kind of play the actor style and the second, the producer-director style.

The Actor Style

The actor style play is by far the more popular with two-year olds and, most of the time, the children choose to be a mother or a father. A first step in pretending to be a mother or father is to dress up in a parent's clothes. As young as eighteen months of age, youngsters love to sneak into their parents' closet or open up all their drawers. They try on hats, shoes, belts and scarves. They adorn themselves with beads and bracelets or cover themselves with makeup. Although this dressing up is highly imitative, the children are beginning to imagine themselves in the parent role.

Another very early way of assuming the parent role is to take care of a baby. The baby can be a stuffed animal, a doll, a puppet, or even a clothespin with a face on it. Like dress-up play, taking care of a baby starts off as imitative but evolves over time into a pretend activity. Almost every family we visited reported at least some caregiving play with a doll, puppet, or stuffed animal. Let's look at three representative scenes.

Heather, at two and a half, had a special corner in her bedroom which served as a dining room table for her baby doll, her Disney World characters and herself. She had the table set for breakfast when we arrived.

"Donald, want juice? I give you juice. Want more juice? Want scrambled egg?" (Heather poured some 'juice' from the pitcher into the cup, and held it to Donald's mouth.)

"Mickey Mouse, you want juice, too, you want egg?" (Heather jabbed the scrambled egg with a fork and brought it up to Mickey's mouth.) Then she turned her attention to the baby dolls.

"Here's bottle, baby doll. All gone, bottle all gone, baby doll." (Heather took the bottle away, placed the doll on her shoulder, and tenderly burped her baby.)

Laura, who is several months younger than Heather, started a caregiving episode by placing herself and Cookie Monster at a small table in the kitchen. First, she fed herself Cheerios with an occasional offering to Cookie Monster. Then she picked up the toy telephone and began to jabber. After several

seconds, Laura put the telephone to Cookie Monster's ear and warned him in a strict voice, "Talk couple few minutes."

Angelina, who is about the same age as Laura, chose Howard Johnson's restaurant to begin her pretend play. While they were waiting for dessert to arrive, Angelina's parents got into a conversation and were not paying attention to her. When they looked up, they discovered that Angelina had placed her Crying Tears doll face down on the table and had removed her clothes. "Clean up, clean up doo," she announced as she wiped Crying Tears' bottom with a paper napkin. After several minutes of vigorous wiping, Angelina unfolded the napkin and covered Crying Tears. "Ah, ah, go sleep," but apparently Crying Tears was not quite ready for sleep. Angelina picked her up suddenly, crunched the napkin and went back to wiping her bottom. "Clean up doo, clean up," she continued in a still louder voice.

These examples of doll play illustrate some typical two year old ideas about the role of a caregiver. Caregivers cook food and feed others, that is, they control the food supply. They diaper babies, wash their faces, brush their hair and are generally responsible for upholding standards of cleanliness.

Finally, caregivers are masters of that wonderful invention, the telephone. Usually they talk on the telephone themselves, but occasionally this privilege is extended to their babies.

As caregivers, two-year olds are also affectionate. They readily hug and kiss their dolls. Interestingly enough, these "children-parents" often are harsh disciplinarians as well. Parents who almost never use spanking as a disciplinary technique may be surprised to see their two-year old energetically spanking a doll.

The children we have described so far played the role of caregiver by animating a doll. Another common way to try out this role is to switch roles with a parent and make the parent be the baby.

"You the baby," Jimmy announced to his father, who had just come from work. "Sit down right here. I bring you drink of juice. You like juice?" Jimmy asked as he fed his father a cup full of air.

"No," his father muttered. "This juice is terrible; it's sour. I want a bunch of grapes."

"Here some grapes," Jimmy continued sweetly, after a quick trip to the hall, which apparently served as a kitchen.

"Oh, brother," his father complained. "These grapes have seeds in them. I think I would like to have some green seedless grapes."

Unperturbed, Jimmy went back to his storehouse in the hall. "Here some gweenless gwapes, Daddy."

Children who take the parent's role may not react so calmly to their demanding babies. Erik decided one evening that he was the mother; and the rest of the family, mother, father, grandma, and grandpa, were all babies. Erik distributed "blankets" to each of his cast and announced, "Bedtime, everybody go to sleep."

"This is no blanket. This is a diaper. I want a blanket," complained Grandpa.

"Okay, you take this blanket," Erik said, pulling away the blanket from his father and giving it to Grandpa.

"I want my blanket back," Erik's father howled in mock rage.

Then his mother joined in. "I want a bigger blanket. This one is too small."

Standing in the middle of the floor with his hands on his hips, Erik said firmly, "Try to be quiet and take your naps."

At two years old, both boys and girls like to play the role of mother. In the same way, girls enjoy playing roles associated with their fathers.

Susan: "Need my lunch box. No butter please — gotta watch my clesteral."

Mother: "Your what? — Oh, your cholesterol — okay, I didn't put any butter on your sandwich." (Hands Susan the empty lunch box.)

Susan: "Bye, going to work — got to hurry." (Gets on Big Wheel and drives from the kitchen to the living room.) "Vroom...vroom...vroom — got to go to work."

Some two-year olds also associate the father role with being the fixer. When we entered Frank's house, he was on the porch inserting the barrel of a toy pistol into a screw head on the window screen. As we watched him, he moved systematically from screen to screen inserting the gun into each screw head and giving it a quick twist. The entire operation was completed without a word. After each of the screws was tightened, Frank went to work on the caulking. Using his gun now as a caulking tool, he went about sealing the cracks in the screens. We asked Frank's mother how this intense interest in fixing got started. It seemed that her own father came to the house about once a month, tool kit in hand, and fixed everything that needed fixing. Frank would trail his grandfather for the entire day cooperating as well as he could in each of the repair jobs. Apparently, Frank had decided that a man's role is to fix things.

Most of the two-year olds in our study reflected conventional stereotypes in their actor-type play. Pretend mothers take care of the home front while

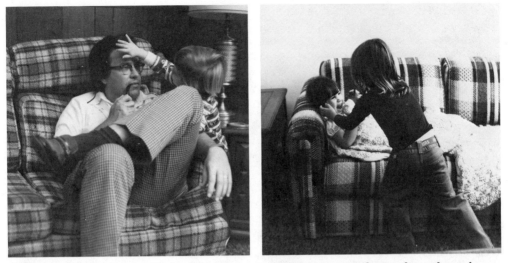

fathers disappear to work. As more parents begin to share the roles of caregiver and provider, the children's ideas undoubtedly will change. However, we expect that two-year olds will continue to understand best the parent roles that are carried out within the home. Because two-year olds are attracted to the home-based behavior of both their mothers and their fathers, it is a good time to provide a variety of props for parent play. Boys enjoy dolls, cooking utensils and tea sets, just as girls enjoy cars, trucks and tool kits.

Next to being a mommy or daddy, the most popular role among two-year olds seems to be pretending to be a doctor. However, the doctor role is too complicated, and perhaps too frightening, for many two-year olds to manage without help from older children and adults. We observed the following example:

Stephanie, a four-year old, picked up her two year old sister and stretched her out on the sofa. "You're the baby and I'm the doctor. I'm gonna make you all better so don't you move." Amy obediently waited while Stephanie poked her with each of the instruments from her doctor kit and gave her several "just pretend" shots. At Stephanie's suggestion, Amy even made pretend crying noises at the appropriate moments. Then, as soon as "Doctor" Stephanie turned her attention elsewhere, Amy took over the doctor role. Her mother was selected as patient and each instrument was used in succession just as she had seen her sister use them. At the end of the examination, Amy gave her mother medicine and an imaginary balloon. The whole procedure had progressed with little conversation, except that Amy provided the appropriate cue when it was time for her patient to cry.

Another role which many of our actor-type children played was being a waiter or waitress. Like doctor play, this pretend theme works best when an adult participates. Andy and his father provided a good demonstration. "I'd

like a large green hot dog with corn ears," requested Daddy. "No man," Andy replied. "We don't got no hot dogs in this restaurant. You want a hamburger?" Father: "No hot dogs! What kind of restaurant is this? Do you have a cucumber and ice cream sandwich?" The game continued with much laughter.

Pretending to be a teacher sometimes appears in the imaginative play of a two-year old. Again, the amount of elaboration depends on the child's familiarity with the role. Theresa had an older sister who was in kindergarten, but she had no idea what really happened there. She did know that her sister took a lunch box to school. Setting Curious George on the kitchen table, she said, "Okay, I'm the teacher. Time for lunch. Open up your lunch box. Eat your lunch right this minute." Tania, a two-year old who went to a small church group three times a week, had a different idea about what teachers do. Like Theresa, she arranged her dolls at the table. "No, no, Baby Boo — no pushin.' How many times I got to tell you? No pushin.' Sit in the corner and don't you move."

In a sense, playing the role of a teacher, a waitress, or a store clerk represents an extension of the caregiver-mother role. The attributes of a caregiver are placed in a new and larger context. In the same way, being a garbage collector or an airplane pilot, which are occasional pretend themes with two-year olds, involves extending the fixer-driver-father role. It seems that two-year olds fall back on the roles they understand best, the roles of mother and father, when they try to play out occupational roles.

Some actor-type children elaborate their imaginative play by taking a different approach. Instead of adapting the parent role to a new identity, they act out unusual events or experiences: a ride on a boat, a trip to the circus, a visit to the beach. With very few exceptions, these imaginary events never reach a culmination. As a matter of fact, most of the time they don't even get off the ground. The high point comes in the preparation.

"Going to the beach," Jennifer announced, as she sorted through the box of stuff in the corner of the room.

"Need the keys. I'm not taking the bus to the beach. Going by car. You want to go to the beach?" she asked her doll, wrapping it in a diaper and stuffing it into the carriage.

"I want to go the beach," Dolly answered in Jennifer's high squeaky voice.

"Wait for me," said Jennifer to the doll. "I've got to get packed up." Jennifer got busy filling a paper bag with an assortment of beach supplies--a toothbrush, a Green Stamp catalogue, an empty milk carton, a string of beads, a piggy bank and a Sesame Street record.

"Got to dress me," she insisted as she struggled to get her arm in the sleeve of a smock. Satisfied with her own outfit, Jennifer found a hat for her doll and a hat for her younger brother. "Want to be the

daddy?" she asked her brother in a solicitous voice.

Jennifer's excursion to the beach never went beyond the packing up stage because the packing up stage became longer and longer. Two-year olds may also extend imaginative play by introducing new events with chaotic rapidity. They skip from theme to theme, and from role to role, with little attention to continuity. Angela provided a delightful example of this kind of versatile play.

When we first came into the house, Angela was riding her giraffe on the back porch. "Hurry up, horsey, hurry up, horsey," she chanted. As soon as she saw us, Angela picked up the horse and carried it into the living room. "Want a drink?" she asked, as she offered the horse a paper cup. Then she turned the horse on its side, felt it to see if it was dry, took its temperature with a spoon, and diapered it with a kitchen towel. When her mother turned on some music, she picked up the horse and danced with it around the room. As the music ended, Angela turned her attention to the horse's wheels. For some reason they reminded her of a barbeque grill. Angela flipped an imaginary hamburger on the grill. "Hungry, Mommy? Want lunch? You want ketchup?"

Producer-Director Style

So far we have been looking at a style of imaginative play in which children are actors, portraying the role of a familiar character or playing out some interesting event. In either situation, they pretend by placing themselves directly in the imaginary scene. Another style of imaginative play that we see during this age is the producer-director style, which is somewhat more detached. The child stands back from the action and directs a pretend world. Sometimes the child animates a cast of miniature characters. At other times, the focus is on arranging an imaginary set. The favorite props for this ac-

tivity are standard commercial toys—cars and trucks, farm animals, Fisher Price people, "Sesame Street" characters, and dollhouse furniture.

Kori had just returned from a trip to Drumland farm. Using a Fisher Price farm set, her mother had prearranged a farm scene on her bedroom floor. Kori examined the scene with intense interest. For several minutes she clutched her hands in a gesture of quiet excitement. "The horse is hungry," Kori's mother suggested. Kori crouched on the carpet. She put the farmer inside the toy wagon and pulled the wagon around in a circle. "You want milk?" she asked the farmer who was driving the wagon. "Hm, thank you — glup, glup, glup," answered the horse. "Want more milk, want some dinner? Pig want milk too?" Kori systematically pulled the wagon around the farm yard, providing the dialogue for the farmer and the animals.

Matthew, like Kori, frequently assumed the producer-director role in an imaginative play routine. He had been playing on the floor with Kermit the frog, a teddy bear and a basketball hoop. When Kermit got stuck in the basketball hoop, his mother initiated the play theme by talking to the frog. "Oh, Kermit, you are hurt. Do you need to go to the doctor?" Matthew immediately answered, "Yes, he's hurt. Take him to the doctor." The doctor conveniently turned out to be Teddy Bear. Matthew gave Kermit "a purple medicine." Next Matthew began to make Kermit move around the room. He described the scene as the action took place. "Now Kermit's leg is all right. He's going to jump over the bed. He's going to jump in the tire—watch this!"

As we examine Kori's orchestration of the Drumland farm scene and Matthew's maneuvers with Kermit the Frog, it is obvious that a good deal of sophistication is needed to verbalize the play ideas of a producer-director. However, two-year olds may set the stage with miniature characters and not add any dialogue. Madeline, who is a relatively nonverbal two-year old, had a package of miniature salt and pepper shakers and a set of tootsie cars. While we were watching, she lined up the cars and put one or two of the shakers beside each car. We weren't sure she was pretending until her older brother asked if he could have a car. Madeline put her arms protectively around the fleet and answered in a cross voice, "No, no! Fill up." "Oh," her brother interpreted. "She's filling her cars with gas."

The producer-director style does not necessarily require miniature people, animals, or elaborate props. It can begin with basic raw materials—blocks, crayons and paper, a ball of clay, or perhaps just words. Once children grasp the idea that they can set the rules in imaginative play and things can become whatever they want them to be, they are ready to devise their own storylines.

Our general impression is that the child who prefers the actor style is physically active, exploratory, energetic and impulsive. The producer-director type is apt to be somewhat more reflective—planning out strategies and developing new ideas. It would be interesting to follow some of these children over time. Will the children who prefer the actor style grow up to be outgoing and social, while the producer-director types grow up to be more reflective and introverted?

Reasons for Pretending

In attempting to describe the various kinds of imaginative play we find in two to three-year olds, we have selected examples that are particularly striking. These examples are not typical of all the families we visited. As a matter of fact, we found many children who were not interested in imaginative play at all. Does imaginative play serve a developmental purpose, and is it a critical factor in social, emotional or cognitive development?

Making Sense Out of the World

As we have already suggested, one reason children pretend is that it helps them make sense out of the world. As children play and replay familiar events, they understand them better. Let us consider once more the ever popular theme of food in the imaginative play of two-year olds. The evolution of this theme will illustrate the link between pretending and the development of new concepts.

At just over a year we see the beginning of pretend eating. One toddler lifts an empty cup to his lips or gives his daddy a pretend bit of dinner; a second toddler makes believe that she is picking a grape off the fruit design on her mommy's blouse. By the middle of the second year, many children have expanded this theme to include the preparation of food. They make cookies out of sand, mix a birthday cake in an empty bowl, or crack pretend eggs on the side of a pan. A further extension, usually in the early two's, involves serving the food. This is the well-known tea party stage, in which the child plays hostess to people, dolls, or stuffed animals.

From this point on, the food theme can be expanded in several directions. Many children at two and a half or three get interested in pretending to buy food at the grocery store. Some children recognize that, before you go to buy

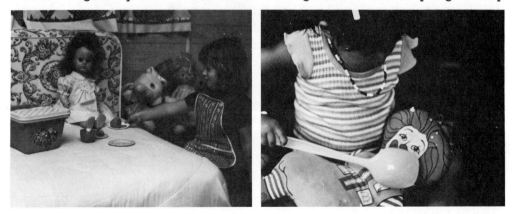

food, you have to make a list of what you need. Other children recognize that you have to get money before you go shopping and so they stop off at the bank on the way to the market. Still other children go on a picnic, plan a barbecue, or eat out in a restaurant.

Looking at the various expansions and extensions of the food theme, we recognize how many different concepts can be associated with it. Two year old children are constantly accumulating additional experience with the process of buying, preparing and eating food. By observing the kind of pretending that a two-year old organizes around food, or any other recurring theme, parents can infer what new ideas are of greatest interest to their child. They are then in a better position to help the child explore and learn about these ideas.

Imaginative play helps two-year olds make sense out of the world on a more abstract level as well. As the children become familiar with a specific imaginary theme, they begin to recognize, at least in that limited context, the difference between reality and fantasy. One indication of this process is the appearance of joking behavior in imaginative play. In the beginning, pretend ideas tend to be carried out in a serious manner. The child who is just learning to set up a tea party or go on an imaginary shopping trip is likely to be quite solemn. But when the pretense becomes well-established, the child becomes more playful. A pretend routine can even become a ritualized joke. Whenever Ken's father sat down to read the newspaper, for example, Ken began a teasing game. Looking at his father and laughing, he would pretend to take huge bites out of his father's tie.

Another sign that children are distingushing between reality and fantasy is the use of the word "pretend." Parents who introduce a word like "pretend" as they play with their two-year olds usually find that their children pick up the term quickly. Once familiar with the term, it becomes easier to discuss situations in which the difference between reality and fantasy is unclear. Imaginary thinking has both power and limitations. It can create a powerful imaginary experience, but not directly change the real world. As children play out a variety of themes, and as parents talk to them about their pretending, children begin to appreciate this paradox.

Compensating for Feelings of Inadequacy

Another explanation for imaginative play is that it provides children with emotional support. At times, children play out scary events until their fears are under control. The kinds of fears that plague the two-year old often appear to be irrational. Parents told us of two-year olds who were afraid of but-

terflies, beards, egg shells, fire sirens, band aids, and Santa Claus. Zachary
would not go to sleep at night because he was afraid that a cow would jump
on the roof and crash into his bedroom.

As we think about the two-year old's growth, we recognize that these fears
are the product of the child's ability to create mental pictures, to imagine
things that are not present. The same developmental advance that gives
children the power to play out imaginary themes also makes them fearful.
They can imagine all sorts of inanimate things coming to life—stuffed animals, trees, the moon, or clothes hanging in the dark.

Gregory was terribly afraid of lions. Several times during the night he would
run into his parents' bedroom, screaming that a lion was after him. At the
same time, he insisted that his mother and father read a story about Johnny
Lion at bedtime. He even took a little stuffed tiger to bed with him at night.
At first glance, it might seem better for Gregory's parents to discourage
reading the book and playing with the tiger. In actuality, this pretending
seems to help Gregory cope with his fear. As he gains experience controlling imaginary lions and tigers, he will be less likely to be plagued by
nightmares.

There usually is a close link between feelings of fear and feelings of excitement. Experiences that are exciting can be frightening as well. Being
pulled in a wagon is great fun up to a certain speed; beyond that, it is terrifying. Being pushed in a swing is tremendously exciting up to a certain

height; beyond that, it too is terrifying. With their new powers of imagination, two year old children can anticipate a fearful situation before it exists. A child who likes dogs but is afraid they will jump on him may begin to whimper at the mere sight of a dog across the street. A child who is interested in fire trucks but afraid of loud noises may become alarmed by the faintest sound of a distant siren. In cases like these, the children's imagination has run away with them and blocked out the excitement of the real situation.

Naturally parents are concerned about the over-reactions of their two-year olds, but this fearfulness is also a sign that the children are ready for more pretending. Imaginative play may tip the balance back in the right direction, from a frightening experience to an exciting one. With the child who cringes at the sight of the neighbor's dog, parents can introduce a stuffed dog who keeps jumping on everyone. The child who cries at the sound of a distant siren can be given a fire truck and parents can play "siren games." "Rrrrrh," the parent wails as the child sits in the bathtub. "Here comes the fire engine to put out a fire." The fire truck roars up the side of the bathtub and along the edge, straight toward the watching child. "Ooops," the parent mutters as the fire truck careens into the bath water. "The fireman had an accident, his siren's broken . . . blub, blub, blub, blub."

Imagination also can deflect feelings of loneliness and insecurity. Almost every two-year old we visited had a favorite doll, stuffed animal, or security blanket. These loved items kept the child company in new and strange situations. At an early age, children are not very selective about the kind of thing they choose for a companion. Several of our young two-year olds were attached to such odd items as screwdrivers, shampoo bottles, or whisk brooms. These objects seemed to be almost animate. The children would insist on taking them along on rides, bringing them to the table, and going to sleep with them. Occasionally parents even heard children talking to these strange companions. "Bye-bye, have to go to store now," Jason said to a new pair of shoes in his closet.

The animation of unlikely objects seems to decline between the ages of two and three, but the animation of dolls and stuffed animals gets even stronger. At Halloween, Erik adopted a large skeleton decoration as his companion. "Look at shoe," he exclaimed with excitement, pointing to the bones in the skeleton's foot. "Mr. Skeleton nice man, he wants eat, too," Erik said. After a large chair had been provided and Mr. Skeleton draped over it, Erik decided that his new companion wanted to eat soap. Later in the day, it looked as if the skeleton had been forgotten on the floor, but Erik informed his parents, "Try to be quiet, Skeleton taking a nap."

Just as pretending can help meet a child's social needs, it can compensate for a child's lack of control over events in the real world. Most of the time, rules are imposed on young children. They are told when to get up and when to sleep, how and what to eat, where to go to the bathroom. The situation is different when two-year olds pretend. They can go on a picnic with "Sesame Street" friends and eat nothing but candy and cookies. They can organize an endless succession of birthday parties or camping trips. They can talk on the phone as long as they want. In imaginative play, the children get to set the rules, boss the characters, and control the outcome.

Ways to Foster Imaginative Play

Among the families we visited, we found very definite attitudes about imagination. In a small minority, imaginative play was frowned upon. It was thought of as a mechanism for avoiding the truth, and children who indulged in imaginative play were scolded for telling lies. A second group of parents, also a minority, tolerated imaginative play but felt that it took away time from more important things like learning numbers and letters. A third group, and by far the majority, felt that imaginative play was important and sought out ways to encourage it. We were especially interested in these families and identified two characteristics these families had in common:

1. There were adults or older children who had a special interest and talent for playing imaginatively with the two-year olds.

2. A variety of materials were available for imaginative play, and parents allowed children to gather their own props and create special places for pretending.

The Role of the Adult

For two-year olds, the greatest inducement for pretending is to play with an adult or older child who enjoys it. As we visited with different families, it was easy to identify the parents who were especially interested in their child's imaginative play. These parents described with obvious pleasure the pretend games they enjoyed with their children.

Brian's family is a clear example of a family that took advantage of their youngster's readiness to play imaginatively. As we walked into the family room, the first thing that caught our eye was a giant wooden structure which took up a good third of the room. This structure was a playhouse built to order by Brian's father. It served as a store, a castle, a jail, a puppet theatre, or just as a good hiding place. Obviously, the family had a great time with it.

Watching parents play with their children, we could see that parents, like children, have a *preferred* style of imaginative play. Some parents prefer to be actors. They participate in a very direct way in their child's pretend themes. Others are definitely the producer-director types, gathering props, suggesting dialogue, drawing pictures, telling stories, or making up rhymes and songs. Finally, we found the "appreciative audience" parents—those who love to watch their children's pretend activities but do not participate very often.

Parents who were skilled in actor-type play knew how to be opportunistic. At just the right moment, they asked a question or made a comment that served to initiate an imaginative play sequence.

Steven was sitting on top of his red car making a "vroom vroom" noise. His father, who had been talking to us, turned to Steven.

"Hello, Mr. Steven. I see you are out in your red Corvette. Are you running a bit low on gas?"

"Filler up please," Steven responded. (Obviously this was not the first time father and son had enacted this scene.)

Steven's father pretended to fill the car with gas. "Do you want me to check the tires? Your right rear looks a bit low on air." Steven watched as his father pretended to check the tires.

Steven: "How much I owe you?"

Steven's father: "Ten dollars even." Steven pretended to take the money out of his pocket and put it in his father's hand. He drove off with a humming sound but was back two minutes later for a repeat performance.

Laura's mother, like Steven's father, very much enjoyed actor-type play. Her particular forte was pantomime. While we were there, she and Laura acted out a pretend game using gestures. Laura was playing in her outgrown cradle which her mother had placed on the floor. As Laura climbed into it, she said, "Boat." Her mother took advantage of the moment. "Let's go on a boat trip," she suggested, climbing in the cradle beside Laura. "We'll see if we can catch a fish. Throw out your rod." At this point Laura's mother went through an elaborate pantomime. She threw out her line, caught a fish, tossed it into the boat, and wiped off the splashes from her face and arms. Laura was very attentive. Obviously, she could not follow the whole routine, but she enjoyed watching her mother's performance.

In many of the homes we visited, an older sister or brother joined in actor-type play. In most cases this worked very well. The two-year old was delighted to be included in the act and was willing to accept any part. Naturally, the younger child was assigned a passive role while the older child provided the leadership, but at the first opportunity the two-year old tried to imitate the more active part. We were amazed at how adept two-year olds could be in following a play routine. Harris, for example, took over the role of teacher when his sister left the room. "This is a A," he told the bionic woman, as he showed her a W. "Say it now, say 'A'. Say 'A' nice and loud so I can hear you."

Many parents who enjoyed being producer-directors helped set up fancy playscapes: a "Sesame Street" playground, a gasoline station, a zoo. Others selected less grandiose stage settings and concentrated their efforts on making puppets or animals talk. Timothy's mother was a most effective director type. She was sensitive to Timothy's inquisitiveness and his interest in replaying a new experience. Timothy had gone on a picnic with his grandfather at a state park. When Timothy came home, he went to the play corner of the family room where all his toys were kept. There, on a low table, he found his little "Sesame Street" people. Big Bird, Ernie and Bert were arranged around a "picnic table," which was a red and white checked paper napkin. Beside the picnic table was a small basket full of bits of junk. Without encouragement, Timothy began to direct the show.

"Want a hamburger, Ernie?" Timothy asked, as he served Ernie a delicious cork coaster. "No, Ernie, no more ketchup. You want ice tea? We don't got ice tea. Want hot dog? Mommy, need cook it." Timothy was now pulling his mommy's jeans.

"Need what?" his mother asked, puzzled by the request.

"Need cook it," Timothy repeated insistently "Need cook it—hot dog."

"Oh, you need to cook your hot dog. You need a barbecue."

"Yes, need cook it."

Timothy was delighted that his mother had understood him. He was perfectly satisfied with the empty juice can she gave him to use as a barbecue.

As we watched Timothy and his mother, it was obvious that this kind of pretending was quite typical. Although Timothy's mother did not get into the act, she knew just which props would get Timothy started. She also accepted Timothy's rules for pretending. Invisible hot dogs were fine to serve to Bert and Ernie as long as they had been cooked on an appropriate grill.

The Props

Whether or not parents are direct participants in an imaginative episode, they play a key role in helping two-year olds find appropriate props. It was interesting for us to see how creative parents became when they got involved in gathering props. For example, we saw three different ways of providing a picnic lunch. One parent filled a picnic basket with pictures of food from a magazine. A second parent filled a shoe box with empty jello, raisin, and cereal boxes. Still another parent used bread dough to make a variety of play foods.

Of course, prop gathering, especially by two-year olds, has drawbacks too. Parents kept telling us about keys, extension cords, credit cards, and pot lids appearing in the oddest places. Typically, these treasures were to be found in a special, private place for pretending. This place, selected by the children, was likely to be too small for adults to enter but just right for small children. Examples that parents mentioned were: under the kitchen sink, behind the sofa, the knee hole of a desk, under a card table with a sheet over it, inside the fireplace, on top of a bunk bed, and under a toddler table.

In order to facilitate prop gathering, we have developed two lists. The first includes props that are most conducive to actor-type play. These props correspond with the different ways children may choose to act out a role.

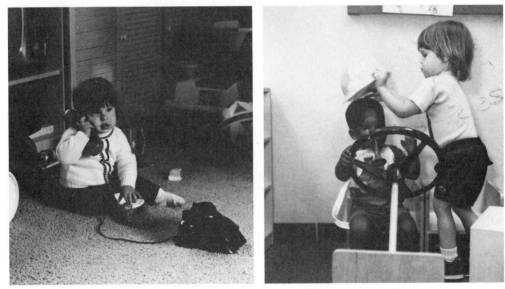

Things to Put On

Hats of all kinds.
Makeup and felt tip markers.
Belts, ties, beads, bracelets, watches.
Grownup shoes, boots, slippers.
Old clothes—smocks, shirts, raincoats.

Places to Go To

Large boxes.
Blankets or sheets that can be thrown over a table to make a tent.
Porches.

Things to Carry

Pocketbooks and billfolds.
Lunch boxes.
Shopping bags.
Suitcases and briefcases.

Things to Use

Toy telephone.
Keys.
Small notebook and pencil.
Bits of string and ribbons.
Dolls, stuffed animals and puppets.
Thermos bottle.
Real or toy pots, pans, dishes, utensils.
Old typewriter or cash register.
Assorted small boxes or containers.
Poker chips, small blocks.
Tongue depressors.
Old photographs.

The second list includes props that especially encourage producer-director type play.

Playscapes

Playhouses, farms, doll houses, restaurants, toy villages, miniature railroads.

Miniature Type Props

Small cars, trucks, and planes.
Fisher Price people, television characters, Disney World characters, small plastic animals.

Raw Materials

Boxes and baskets.
Squares of fabric, linoleum, tile or rugs.
Blocks.
A heavy tag board or plywood square to use as a roof or floor.
Crayons, watercolors, and inexpensive paper.
Chalkboard and chalk.
Flannel board or colorform sets.

*   *   *

We have looked in a systematic way at the ingredients of pretend play—the interested parent, the appropriate props, the special play space. But even with these ingredients, imaginative play cannot flower without a foundation of real world experiences. The more meaningful experiences children have, the greater their potential for play. Sometimes we see parents substitute toys for experience. By filling the child's room with every possible toy, these parents develop a sense of security about their child's development.

A toy is a replication of a real world thing but, if children have not experienced the real world, they have difficulty with the analogy. Most of the important experiences for two-year olds are the everyday routine events—getting dressed, eating, cleaning up, going to the grocery store, taking a bath. Some important experiences are out of the ordinary events—a trip to the zoo, an airplane ride, a Thanksgiving dinner. Still other important experiences come from television and books.

The emergence of imaginative play in two-year olds is an exciting phenomenon, but it needs to be put in proper perspective. The children are just beginning to take advantage of the potential of pretending. Their imaginative play is not yet very sophisticated. They pack up for a trip to the beach and never leave the house. They feed the dolls a birthday cake and then blow out the candles. Most of their pretend themes are simple and cannot be elaborated without help from older people. In fact, quite a few two-year olds do minimal pretending. In some cases, they are busy with other developmental tasks, mastering motor skills, manipulating objects, and interacting with different people. In other cases, they do not yet have the verbal skills to extend an imaginary theme. Whatever the reason for their lack of pretending, it is not irreversible. With time and parental support, all children can reap the benefits of imaginative play, extending the boundaries of space and time, experiencing new powers, and exploring their own creativity.

Chapter 6
EXPLORATIONS

Lisa looked up quickly as her mother entered the bedroom.

"Lisa, what are you doing with that good perfume? Oh, no! You naughty girl! You poured it all out."

Lisa's mother was too upset to explain her feelings any further. She gave Lisa a good spanking and sent her to her room. "Things like this always seem to happen when I'm on the phone," she thought. "And why didn't I have the sense to put that perfume in a safer place?"

Exploration means playing with objects and learning about them in the process. As soon as they are able, children start to explore the world by manipulating the objects around them. Their ability to explore grows as they become stronger, more coordinated, and more determined. By the age of two, most children are not easily deterred from their goals. Lisa wanted to play with the perfume, and she knew exactly when to go into her mother's bedroom and how to get up on the dresser. It was hard to get the little cap unscrewed, but her perseverance was rewarded.

There are moments when every parent is upset by a child's exploration. It seems that exploration always means playing with things that are off-limits. It certainly is true that two year old children tend to be most interested in the very objects with which they are not allowed to play. Lisa's mother was particularly angry because she felt her daughter knew better than to play with the perfume, and that her behavior was an act of defiance.

The exploration of two-year olds can turn into defiance. The children are sophisticated enough to tease a parent, or even to get back at a parent, by getting into things they shouldn't. In extreme cases, children are involved continually in this kind of rebellion. They see the world in terms of confrontation, and they build up their sense of accomplishment by breaking the limits set by parents.

However, not all inappropriate exploration is an expression of defiance. Lisa may merely have succumbed to temptation, as we all do at times. Perhaps she was trying to imitate her mother by putting on some perfume. A forbidden object often is explored not so much because it is forbidden but because it represents a chance to imitate adults, to participate in the grown-up world.

Exploration has two faces. When we look at it one way, we see the possibility of conflict between children and parents as they clash over restric-

tions and rules. When we look at its other face, we see the possibility of cooperation as children learn from their parents how to master certain manipulative skills. Use of the perfume bottle may become a recurring battle at Lisa's house, or it may become a learning opportunity. Perhaps Lisa can put on a drop of perfume while her mother supervises, or perhaps she can have her own bottle of inexpensive perfume to put on when she wishes.

Whether exploration leads to confrontation or cooperation depends on children as well as parents. Some children are especially independent, active, or curious. Some children don't understand verbal explanations their parents give them about the rules for exploration. The situation is different in every family. There is no one way for parents to substitute cooperation for confrontation and, even if families are relatively successful in avoiding confrontation, situations will always arise in which there is no way to avoid it. A certain amount of conflict over exploration is inevitable.

There is a subtle but unmistakable difference in emphasis between the exploration of the one to two-year old as against the two to three-year old. By two years, children are less concerned with experimentation and more concerned with mastering skills. Instead of trying a whole bag of manipulative tricks on an object, the two year old child practices skills associated with that object. Kim, for example, was very interested in exploring her mother's lipstick. Most of the time she did not try to squash the lipstick, break it into pieces, or smear it on the walls. Instead she practiced making the lipstick go up and down in the tube and spreading it on her lips.

In this chapter, we will look at the nature of two-year old exploration from several different perspectives: visual exploration, filling and emptying, drawing and building, finding out how things work, and moving through space. In reality, these perspectives overlap, and the objects that give rise to the greatest exploration are those that lend themselves to more than one kind of exploration. But regardless of how an object is explored, the ultimate goal is mastery, and two year old children look to their parents to help them reach this goal.

Visual Exploration

Looking for Things

When we think about the exploration of two-year olds, we get a picture of incessant activity, running from one room to another, jumping on the bed, piling toys in the middle of the room. Exploration is all of this, but it is also more. Even when young children are sitting quietly, they are usually exploring the world with their eyes. They are not involved in mental reflection, as adults often are, but are very much tuned in to the immediate environment.

Visual exploration occurs all the time, but it is most noticeable when children are restricted from moving around. The outstanding example is riding in the car. "I see a crane. Boy, that's a big one! Pow! Splash!" Stuart described the sound of the crane's bucket hitting the water as it dipped to scoop up another load of gravel. When Stuart rode in the car, he was happy as long as a crane could be found every ten minutes or so. Luckily, there were a lot of gravel pits in the neighborhood.

Many children are like Stuart in that they look for particular objects while riding in the car. Helaine looked for cement mixers; Jennifer looked for big trees; Erik looked for fireboxes. This kind of behavior is one indication of how the exploration of the toddler turns into a sense of mastery in the two-year old. Instead of just watching the scenery go by, the children try to master the visual environment by actively searching for favorite sights. And like Stuart, if the scenery becomes too dull, the children lose interest in visual exploration. They lose the sense of being in control.

Searching for special objects also involves matching. The children are taking into account the similarities between objects. Matching is prominent at the dinner table where two-year olds are more or less confined to their chairs. One night when company was coming, Jeff's mother set the table with dark green glasses, thinking that Jeff would be happy to get an adult glass instead of his usual plastic one. But Jeff was not fooled so easily. "I want beer," he announced as soon as the meal began. The white liquid in his glass obviously did not match the bubbly stuff in everyone else's glass.

Matching often is stimulated by a negative presence, something undesirable that the child wants to avoid. Susan demonstrated her matching skill by fishing out the peas in her vegetable soup and dropping them ceremoniously on the floor. Chris, who was distressed about a hole in his pocket, checked all his other pockets, as well as his father's pockets, to see if they had holes. Erik did not like the way the label in one of his shirts rubbed against his neck. His mother would not agree to ruin the shirt by cutting out the label, even though Erik showed her the offensive labels in all his other shirts.

Watching for Changes

A number of parents reported that their children were interested in watching the sky. The sky is relatively uncluttered and this may be why two year old children are attracted to it. Perhaps it is simply the majesty of the sky. In any event, there are interesting objects in the sky. Two-year olds are like toddlers in that they watch the movements of birds and airplanes. In addition, many of them become attentive to clouds, the sun and the moon.

A favorite spot for watching the sky seems to be sitting on a swing. Most two-year olds have not really learned to pump the swing and, as an adult pushes them, they have ample opportunity for sky gazing. Swinging higher and higher, it must seem as if they are actually going up to meet the sky. Looking down is interesting, too, especially on a sunny day. "I see the shadow," Nicole chanted to herself. "Where you go, shadow?" she playfully mused, as the shadow passed out of sight beneath her feet. As it appeared on the backswing, "I see you now, you silly shadow."

Shadows are mysterious phenomena that are very intriguing to children. They change their shapes on walls, grow long at night, and disappear altogether on some days. But they make good companions, always ready to play "Follow the Leader" and always right in step.

The world is full of physical changes that we take for granted but which two year old children see as fresh and exciting. One of the most common, and yet still fascinating, is the movement of water down a drain. The water seems to move with a will of its own, carrying along an entourage of bubbles and bits of debris. Dropping a stone in a pool of water is similar. At first there is an interesting sound, a "pfloop," and then the rock disappears, swallowed up in a pattern of ripples.

Melting is another surprising event. Stephanie watched some ice cubes disappear in her bowl of soup. Ice cubes in soup was a ritual at her house ever since the first time Stephanie had burned her mouth on hot soup. Now Stephanie asked for the ice even when she didn't want to eat the soup. Andrew watched a burning candle fill up with melted wax which then dripped slowly down the side. From repeated burnings, the base of the candle looked like a multicolored waterfall. Andrew wanted to touch the wax as it assumed its new shape at the bottom of the candle, but he had learned from past experience just to watch.

Probably the most dramatic physical change two-year olds watch is bleeding. Suddenly, bright red liquid covers the skin, emerging effortlessly from a break that often is not visible. Many children eventually develop a fear of blood, but more frequently the reaction among two-year olds is one of fascination. As Jenny exclaimed when she saw the blood from a cut on her leg, "What is *that*?" She wanted to know where it came from and listened attentively to a brief description of her insides. Thinking that her father would be just as overwhelmed by the discovery of blood, she kept telling her mother all afternoon, "I want to show Daddy when he gets home."

Not as dramatic, but still interesting, is the scab formed by dried blood. Two year old children are forever on the lookout for scratches and scrapes on themselves and other people. Scabs are special body parts that come and go. Each one serves as a conversation piece for a few days and then fades away.

In discussing visual exploration we have described only a few of the interesting sights that young children notice and comment on. These examples are not meant to suggest that two year old children are supposed to notice such things. Every child sees something different. However, two-year olds do have in common certain visual abilities. They can search actively for favorite objects; they are aware of interesting movements and physical transformations going on around them; and they like to match and generalize. The exciting part for parents is to watch what their children see in the world and to share in the sense of discovery.

Often parents can suggest a new watching activity. Jason was interested in the contrast between light and shadow. One night, after watching slides,

his father showed him a shadow game. He held Jason's teddy bear in front of the light from the projector and a teddy bear shadow appeared on the screen. Jason got the idea and tried casting shadows of his other toys. Jon's mother suggested a watching activity by giving Jon a flashlight in a dimly lit room. The spot of light was like a live thing, and Jon and his mother enjoyed describing its antics: "It's flying up to the ceiling! Look, the light is jumping on the piano! Oh, it's sleepy, it's lying on the floor."

Filling and Emptying

Exploring Containers

One of the preferred pastimes of toddlers is emptying: bookcases are cleared, milk is poured on the floor, waste-baskets are overturned. Two-year olds continue and expand upon this theme. Taller, stronger, and more agile, they can get into heavy drawers, open closet doors, and climb up to high shelves. As Amy's mother described it, "Amy has graduated to drawers and linen closets." Because of a child's passion for emptying, particular spots in the house may be "out of order" for a while.

In general, however, the emptying behavior of two-year olds differs in characteristic ways from that of toddlers. Emptying for its own sake diminishes. Instead, emptying is often part of a larger plan. The children are looking for specific objects, and emptying simply represents the fastest way to search. When she emptied the dressers, Amy was looking for her mother's makeup

and jewelry.

In many cases, emptying serves as a prelude to filling. Most two-year olds are engrossed in mastering the skills involved in filling, which usually is more acceptable than emptying. Filling behavior is stimulated by interesting containers. Christopher was not the only child we observed packing and unpacking an old purse. He talked to himself about his work. "Put it straight – crayons fit – hope this fits, too." Purses have several advantages. They are important adult objects, they are a challenge to open and close, and they can be carried around when full. The world is full of other interesting containers: small suitcases, shopping bags, crayon boxes, plastic bottles, milk cartons, envelopes. New opportunities are discovered all the time.

Just as a special container stimulates filling and emptying, so does an unusual content. Two year old children enjoy filling a container with small items, such as pieces of macaroni, pennies, shells, pebbles, or buttons. By far the most intriguing material is liquid. Here again we see the change in emphasis from experimentation to mastery. Toddlers love to pour out cups of water, milk, juice, or other liquids. With two-year olds, the emphasis is on

pouring liquid *into* a cup or other container. Parents repeatedly told us about two-year olds getting into the refrigerator in order to pour a glass of refreshment for themselves. This activity was both an exciting way to fill a container and an important way to express independence, and the children were quite upset when their parents tried to take over.

A two-year old's ability to fill containers with water can become an obsession when the child learns to turn on faucets. B.J. was constantly at the kitchen sink trying to fill a glass with water. For several months, Erik spent his bathtime draining the tub and then refilling it. Jodi liked to sneak into the bathroom and fill the sink until it overflowed.

Filling and emptying containers of water is a theme with many variations. Chad watered the plants outside with a hose, filling up the pots with water and watching it sink out of sight. Brian, who had learned to pour water from a sprinkling can, enjoyed sprinkling his parents when they took a bath. Kori found a unique way to fill a pan with water, squatting in the snow and catching the drops from a melting icicle.

Two-year olds play with sand and mud much as they do with water. Containers are filled and then poured out. Under the tutelage of adults, the children may help make a sand cake or a mud pie but, in general, the focus is not on construction. Instead, children are caught up in manipulating these elusive materials and experiencing their peculiar qualities.

Puzzles

Puzzles represent a kind of container that must be filled in a precise way. Shape sorters are a popular version with two-year olds. One of Brandon's favorite playthings was a shape sorting toy in the form of a cash register. Brandon never tired of putting the three different shapes in their respective holes. We watched Mary play with a more complicated version, the Tupperware Ball. Not only were there more shapes to recognize, but fitting the shapes into the holes required careful orientation. The hexagonal piece, for example, would not fit through the hexagonal hole unless it was turned in just the

right way. Mary had learned to place the piece against the hole and rotate it slowly. Sometimes this strategy worked and sometimes it didn't, but Mary was very patient and eventually all the pieces were inside.

Two-year olds are interested in inset puzzles. Heather showed us how she could complete a letter puzzle. Like the shape-sorting toys, the puzzle was relatively simple in that each hole could be filled independently. In other words, each piece was a separate puzzle. Single piece puzzles, such as Heather's letter puzzle, help children solve the orientation problem. Heather was familiar with the normal orientation of the letters so she knew how to turn the puzzle pieces in order to make them fit. Heath and Colby, twins who had just turned three, were interested in multi-piece wooden puzzles. Solving this kind of puzzle was considerably more difficult. Each piece that was fit into the puzzle affected the placement of other pieces, and the orientation of the pieces was not always obvious.

What is most striking is the ability of two year old children to memorize puzzle solutions. Even before children can solve the problem of a shape-sorting toy, they have memorized what shape goes in what hole. They quickly learn where each piece belongs in an inset puzzle. Completing a multi-piece puzzle is primarily a feat of memory. The child has memorized the location of the pieces, the orientation of each piece, and the sequence for inserting the pieces.

Children often demonstrate that they have memorized a puzzle solution by initiating some kind of game. Kelly asked her mother to guess which pictures were painted under the pieces in the farm puzzle. Erik played a "no" game. Holding a piece that was clearly wrong over a hole in the puzzle, he asked, "Think that will fit?"

Two-year olds enjoy playing the role of teacher and showing their parents how to solve a puzzle. Puzzles can sometimes be frustrating, however, and parents may be able to alleviate this frustration. With a child who is just beginning to play with multi-piece puzzles, parents can introduce the idea of removing only one or two puzzle pieces at a time and then fitting them back in: "Let's see. I think I'll take out the dog's head and this wheel here. See if you can put them back in. Now, what do you want to take out?" If children want to remove all the pieces from a puzzle, parents can help them get started by suggesting that they look for a piece with a particualr detail or color. Sometimes parents can actually find the piece and then let the child figure out how it fits in.

Probably the most valuable assistance parents can provide is to help two-year olds pick up their puzzles after playing with them and put them in a place where they will not be disturbed. We visited several homes in which puzzle pieces were scattered loose in the closet or at the bottom of a toy box. Puzzles in this condition are of little use to children.

Drawing and Building

Drawing

When we arrived at John's house, his mother told us that John really "had a thing" about smiley faces. He practiced drawing them on every possible occasion. A little while later we went outside and John quite spontaneously confirmed his mother's statement. He picked up a chunk of limestone from the driveway and used it to draw a perfectly recognizable smiley face in the middle of the sidewalk. As John sat back to admire his product, it was obvious that he was not just exploring the properties of the limestone. He was interested in the fact that he had created a face.

Occasionally, the two-year old begins with the notion of drawing a particular object, as with John and his smiley faces. More frequently, the two-year old begins by making the drawing and the identification comes afterwards. After scribbling with a blue crayon, Jodi looked at her drawing and said, "Look at the blue doggy Jodi made." Often the same object reappears in different scribbles. Nicole saw elephants and triangles, Jamie saw suns and moons, Matthew saw bananas and apples. The tendency to see things in a scribble is encouraged by adults, but it is such a persistent phenomenon that it seems to spring primarily from the perception of the child. Many times, but not always, there really is a form in the scribble that suggests the object the child names.

The drawing of most two-year olds may lack planning but it does not lack structure. There are discernible elements in this scribbling. One child may make circular scribbles while another makes jagged up and down lines that look something like a picket fence. In addition, two-year olds often distinguish between drawing and writing elements. Matthew, for example, drew either big circles or teeny closed shapes. Lisa created circles or half inch long lines. Shawn made either line scribbles or little chicken scratches. These children reported objects in their larger drawings, but words in their little scribbles.

Usually two-year olds use a small number of colors in each drawing. Their use of color seems to change as they become more familiar with a particular medium. Children who are just starting to use crayons tend to complete a scribble with one crayon, while those with several months' experience begin to combine colors. When watercolors or tempera are first used, the children may go through a period in which a blob of a single color is created. Later on, a variety of shapes and colors becomes more likely. The preferred medium for many children is the felt tip pen. Felt tips combine a fine point for easy scribbling with the vivid color of paints.

It comes as quite a revelation to young children that representational objects can be drawn. Children in our culture are surrounded by pictures and they learn to recognize pictures at an early age. It is usually considerably later, however, that they realize pictures can be drawn. Many of the two-year olds in our study were so captivated by this discovery that they asked their

parents to draw for them.

Although parents often express embarrassment over their own artistic skills, two-year olds are not a critical audience. Once parents take the plunge and start to draw, both parents and children enjoy themselves. A parent whose drawing is a bit rusty can begin with simple objects, like chocolate chip cookies or ice cream cones, and then work up to fire engines and bears. The objective is not to teach young children to draw, but to respond to their interests, to follow a line of exploration they cannot pursue by themselves.

Some two-year olds like to "erase" drawings. Andy, for example, after asking his mother to draw garbage trucks, would color all over the picture. Andy did not seem to be trying to destroy the drawing so much as to participate in its creation. Frequently, two-year olds respond in this way to coloring books. They scribble over the pictures without the slightest concern about using "proper" colors. The printed pictures inspire the children to experiment with their own artistic skills.

Some people worry that exposing children to adult drawing, or giving them coloring books, will stunt their artistic development. Our experience indicates just the opposite. Two year old children welcome outside stimulation, as long as it is presented casually. Feelings of inferiority arise only when adults set artistic standards for children and try to teach them to draw.

When children first discover they can create marks, there tends to be an outbreak of scribbling on walls and furniture. Each time a new discovery is made, another burst of intense activity is likely and the drawing may show up in the wrong place. Daryl's mother was surprised one day to see scribbling on Daryl's bedroom wall because she thought he had finished with that long before. She was about to scold him when she noticed that the scribbles were a first attempt to write the letters of his name. Lisa, who had given up drawing on walls, discovered she could decorate herself. For several weeks afterwards, her arms, legs, and stomach were covered with artwork. These periods of over-exuberant drawing usually pass quickly, as the child's desire to explore a new discovery becomes satiated.

Building

As in drawing, the building efforts of the two-year old show a distinct developmental progression. The toddler's energy seems to go primarily into knocking down towers that have been built by other people. However, toddlers are also developing important construction skills. They stack objects on top of one another and they lay out toys in rows. In doing so, they are learning about two important building principles: balance and straight lines.

These ideas are explored further between the ages of two and three. Towers become taller and children discover how to make them both more stable

and more pleasing to the eye. One method is to build a tower with objects that are of similar size and shape. When Trevor was given a set of blocks with different shapes, he intentionally stacked squares together, circles together, and triangles together, creating columns that were solid and attractive. Younger children sometimes utilize this principle, but more often their stacking is haphazard.

A second and more sophisticated way to design a tower is to place the larger shapes on the bottom and the smaller, less regular shapes on the top. This idea seems patently obvious to us as adults, but children do not learn it for some time. Toddlers try to balance the most unlikely combinations—a frisbee on top of a toy school bus, which is on top of a peanut butter jar. This kind of wild experimentation declines among two-year olds as they learn to balance smaller objects on top of a larger base.

Whether the tower of a two-year old looks like a smooth column, a delicate turret, or just a random collection, it usually is labeled. Jennifer, for example, considered her towers to be churches and castles. Beverly built a tall tower and described it as the office "where Daddy lives." Similar to the drawings of two-year olds, constructions like these are hardly realistic, but the children have gained the insight that a real object can be symbolically represented by a set of blocks.

Just as towers get taller, lines get longer and they also begin to represent something else. Matthew lined up all his toy animals on the back of the sofa and called it a bridge. Colby made long lines of blocks and referred to them as trains. Michael put his Fisher Price people in a row and pretended it was a parade. As these examples illustrate, two-year olds are not limited to building lines with blocks. A line can be created with puzzle pieces, silverware, or beads on a string.

Sooner or later, the two-year old who is interested in building lines makes a major discovery: the corner. Once corners become a possibility, many different kinds of flat constructions can be built with line elements. A line can change direction, two lines can intersect, a line can keep turning until it forms an enclosure. With just a few suggestions or demonstrations, two-year olds make a host of imaginary objects: fences, roads, beds, dance floors and swimming pools.

The role of parents in building activities, as in drawing activities, is to strike a balance between demonstrating new ideas and allowing children to work on their own. Building a tower with a new element, such as a cross bar that becomes an imaginary diving board, may stimulate imitative efforts by a two-year old. Building a simple network of roads may trigger more elaborate block play. The particular forms made by parents are inconsequential, for the goal is not to teach techniques of block building. The goal is to support two year old children as they explore building possibilities, and to share in their sense of discovery. The fun comes not just in the building, but in the conversation and imaginary play that follows.

Traditional construction toys, such as Tinker Toys and Lincoln Logs, are designed for children older than three. They require greater coordination and dexterity than the two-year old possesses. However, the tinker toy idea, fitting a peg in a hole, does appeal to two year old children, and there are versions that are satisfactory.

Interlocking blocks, like Lego, also are available for building tower constructions. This type of toy is less flexible than a set of wooden blocks, but

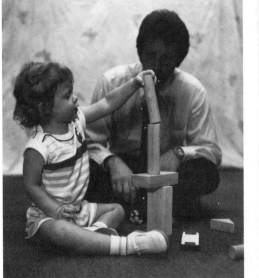 

it may give the child a feeling of having built something more substantial. With any of these construction toys, two-year olds seem to be primarily interested in learning how to connect the pieces, and less attention is paid to experimenting with different forms.

Arts and Crafts

Arts and crafts projects represent a kind of activity related to drawing and building. In general, these projects are beyond the capacities of a two-year old. Beverly's mother regularly helped her do arts and crafts projects from a "Sesame Street" magazine, but she began to sense that Beverly was being pushed too hard. Beverly started to complain, "I can't," whenever her mother suggested a new project.

Arts and crafts are most effective when older children are included. Even so, the focus of the two-year old is on manipulating the material more than on creating a product. Playing with clay is a good example. Two year old children occasionally create a clay product such as a cake, a hamburger, or a snake. For the most part, they enjoy pounding, squeezing, and poking the clay and, if left alone, invariably end up tearing the clay into little pieces and throwing it around the room. Then the only end product is a mess to be cleaned up. Many of the families we visited were not enthusiastic about letting their two-year olds play with clay or playdough. Apparently, the parents thought the inconvenience outweighed the possible benefits.

Most two-year olds do not have the skill to use paper as a medium for craft projects either. If they can use scissors at all, it is simply to cut a large piece of paper into smaller pieces. Smearing glue around is fun for a few minutes, but most of it ends up in the wrong place and the children get discouraged.

We did notice that two year old children created their own version of cutting and pasting. For example, eating toast became a craft project for Matthew. He "cut" the material by taking a bite of toast. Then he looked at the remaining bread to see what it resembled. Michael saw letters and numbers in half-eaten pretzels. Examples of "pasting" projects were even more common. Erik stuck a dozen pieces of scotch tape on his broken fire hat. Jodi sneaked into the bathroom and covered herself with bandaids. Amy stuck pencils into a ball of clay. Brian planted twigs in the dirt.

These examples are typical of the two-year old's orientation. The emphasis is on manipulation, on the process of tearing apart or sticking together. Occasionally a product may result, but it is more of a coincidence than a planned outcome.

Finding Out How Things Work

Machines

The preeminent machine in our culture is the automobile. From an early age, most children want to operate this machine. Between the ages of two and three, a child may learn to insert the ignition key, honk the horn, and turn on the lights, the wipers and the car radio. The outstanding aspect of pretend driving, though, is turning the steering wheel. Two-year olds want to steer all kinds of vehicles, the tractor lawn mower in a department store, the bulldozer sitting idle in the vacant lot next door, the neighbor's motor-cycle. Marcie, for example, was trying to steer her uncle's new car. She voiced the sentiment of many two-year olds when she said, "This car is mine."

Children also adopt secondary roles when denied a primary role in op-erating a machine. Most of the time they cannot operate the steering wheel of the family car but they can assume other roles. Lisa unbuckled her seat

belt every time the car stopped at a traffic light, at the drive-up bank, or at a toll booth. Naturally she did not like to be restrained, yet there was more than a dislike of restraint in her behavior. As soon as the car started again, she wanted to fasten her seat belt, much to the frustration of her mother. Controlling the seat belt was Lisa's way of participating in the operation of the car. Angie, who was always asking if she could steer the car, settled for opening the car door by herself. Jason took charge of pushing down the lock buttons on all the doors.

Two-year olds are likely to be fascinated by car junkyards, if they have a chance to see them. Benjie and Jamie, two brothers we visited, had an ideal situation from this standpoint. Their father salvaged parts off old vehicles, and over a dozen cars and boats were parked around the house. There was no problem in sharing. While Jamie steered a grounded motorboat, Benjie

drove a wrecked Volkswagen. It was a two-year old's dream-come-true.

Many of the exciting machines in a child's environment are electrical. The television set is a case in point. With a push of a button, the dark screen is transformed into a talking picture. Many of the two-year olds we visited were discouraged from touching the television set, but most of them had still learned how to turn it on and off.

Stereos present a similar situation. Two-year olds usually are trained to stay away from them and do not know much about operating them. Telephones are a bit more accessible. Like B.J., many two-year olds have mastered the art of dialing and it is only a matter of time before they make a connection with a distant party. B.J.'s telephone was also installed on a jack, which he soon learned to unplug. When he wasn't dialing strangers, he was carrying around a disconnected phone. The push button telephone, which has become common, is even more fun for children because each number emits a distinct tone when pressed.

The list of machines in which a two-year old may become interested is endless. Parents told us of children wanting to operate slide projectors, hairdryers, blenders, lawn mowers, garage door openers, electric typewriters, sewing machines and power drills. Two year old children are attracted to machines because they are important adult objects. Operating a machine is not only a privilege; it often is a way of expressing adult-like power. Chopping food in the blender, or opening the heavy garage door, is an impressive act. It makes the children feel they have caused a powerful change.

Frequently these machines are either too dangerous or too valuable for children to explore, and a power struggle ensues. In deciding how to handle the desire of two-year olds to operate machines, the practical orientation of the children should be kept in mind. The overriding goal of a two-year old is simply to turn on the machine, to make something exciting happen. No great intellectual damage results if children are forbidden to touch the television or stereo. They would not be learning much about electricity in any case. On the other hand, if children are allowed to operate a machine, they may soon master the process and grow tired of it. Instead of dragging on for months, or even years, the conflict over a particular machine may be dissipated in a short time.

Each situation is different. Sometimes children are satisfied with the appearance of operating a machine. Mary was content to play with an extra telephone that was left unplugged. It never rang and had no dial tone, but that did not bother her. Sometimes parents can supervise children while they explore a machine. Colby and Heath were allowed to use the garage door opener under supervision. Erik could operate the slide projector as long as his father gave him guidance. In some cases young children get so proficient that they are able to operate a machine without assistance. Jed, for example, handled the vacuum cleaner by himself.

With electrical machines, there still is the problem of plugging the equipment in. Nearly all the children in our study were interested in puttings plugs into wall outlets, and nearly all the parents did not think their children were old enough to learn this skill. Although some of the children accepted their parents' admonitions, others paid no attention. Putting covers on the outlets did not help because the children were old enough to pry them off.

When children insist on acquiring this skill, despite warnings, threats and spankings, it seems advisable to help them learn. Mary's parents had taught her the first step in learning how to handle plugs—taking a plug out. She was allowed to unplug cords, but not to plug them back in. So far this compromise has worked. Shawn's parents have gone a step further. They finally agreed to let Shawn put plugs in the outlet while they were watching. Nothing had discouraged him from trying on his own, including several shocks. In fact, Shawn was so intrigued by electricity that a favorite comment was, "Let's talk about plugs." Then he would point out different plugs in the house and expect his mother to elaborate on this engrossing subject.

Mechanical Toys

The major way we handle the desire of two-year olds to operate machines is to give them toy substitutes. Nearly every two-year old has a toy telephone to compensate for not being allowed to play with the real one. We give young children toy radios, cameras, record players and even television sets. From an adult viewpoint, these substitutions are often rather pathetic as machines, but most two-year olds seem happy as long as a toy telephone makes a little jingle or a toy radio plays a simple tune.

When we visited Laura, she showed us her record player. As soon as one record began, she stopped it and turned it over, or else put on another record. Manipulating the record player was more fun than listening to the music. The same thing happened with the viewmaster. The excitement lay in putting the discs in the machine and pressing the advance mechanisms. The pictures themselves drew only a passing glance.

Two year old children are interested in a variety of other mechanical toys. We noticed several children who had renewed their interest in the Jack-in-the-Box toy they had received as babies. Now they could operate the toy, push the clown down inside, close the lid and turn the crank. In a similar way, we saw children winding up musical stuffed animals that had been with them since infancy. Busy-boxes were once again appealing because this time the child could easily manipulate the mechanisms and study the cause and effect relationships. There were new mechanical toys as well. Wind-up vehicles could be activated. Toys that worked according to air pressure could be made to jump. Spring-loaded toys could be operated successfully. These mechanical toys stimulate the same pattern of behavior as adult machines. An intense burst of interest is likely as the child seeks to master the skill involved in making the toy work. Once this skill is developed and the child has practiced it sufficiently, the toy loses its appeal and starts to gather dust.

Tools

Two year old children are interested in tools for much the same reason as machines. Tools are associated with adults and they can be used to make something happen. In fact, tools are a kind of machine and many modern tools are electrical. But even the traditional, non-electrical tools are favorites with two year old children. They try to mop the floor, rake the yard, sweep the steps, and dig a hole in the garden. Once again, manipulating the tool is more important than the quality of the outcome.

Between the ages of two and three, many children are allowed to handle hammers, screwdrivers and wrenches. Although toy tools are available, real ones are often easier to use. The children are most successful at hammering. Benjie and Jamie helped their father hammer out pieces of copper tubing from old air conditioners. Each boy had his own hammer and could spend as long as he liked pounding on the tubing.

Some children are unusually skilled with tools. We watched Frank, who

was three years old, drive a nail, try to cut a wire with a set of pliers, and start to pry off a hubcap with a screwdriver. His mother described how Frank always took things apart. He removed the cork seals from around the windows. His favorite toy was a truck that could be reduced to pieces. He crushed his food to bits at the table. In fact, one of the most exciting experiences of his life had been helping his grandfather take the dishwasher apart.

The outstanding function of many tools is to take things apart, and this is the characteristic that children seize on. Children like Frank, who are especially interested in mechanical relationships, will be more destructive. Shawn, for example, went beyond most children in investigating how the toilet worked. Not content to just learn how the toilet was flushed, he kept removing the back and tinkering with the mechanism inside. When a child shows a strong inclination to take things apart, one idea is to provide an "explorer" box full of objects that can be dismantled. Of course, someone has to put them back together if they are to be used again.

Even children who are not proficient with tools are interested in the process of taking things apart. Heather was adept at peeling a tangerine. Angela enjoyed unsnapping clothes and unzipping zippers. Mary kept breaking off the figurines in a shadow box and asking her mother to glue them back. She was not the only child we saw who played the game of "I break it – you fix it."

Moving Through Space

Exploration With Movement

Exploration is active: it involves movement. We already have described some of the ways two-year olds move objects as they explore them. Puzzle pieces are rotated until they fit, blocks are arranged to make an enclosure, a hammer is swung against a wooden peg. These are movements on a relatively small scale.

Movement on a larger scale is more characteristic of two-year olds. Even when exploring a puzzle, a set of blocks or a toy workbench, they are up and down, circling around – now squatting, now standing, now running to the window. Movements of the whole body represent an important part of exploration. The children are discovering the possibilities and limitations of their own bodies, and at the same time they are learning about the space that surrounds them.

Toddlers are interested in testing themselves against large and cumbersome objects. They strain to push, pull and lift these obstacles. Two-year olds continue this kind of body exploration, although their interest seems to be waning. The primary mode of the active two-year old is no longer pushing or carrying, but running. Children at this age are inveterate runners. They are willing to run even when they are too tired to walk. However, the racing technique of older children has not been mastered yet. Two-year olds may run with gusto, but their short, choppy steps go nowhere fast. And trying to turn a sharp corner often results in an abrupt and painful landing.

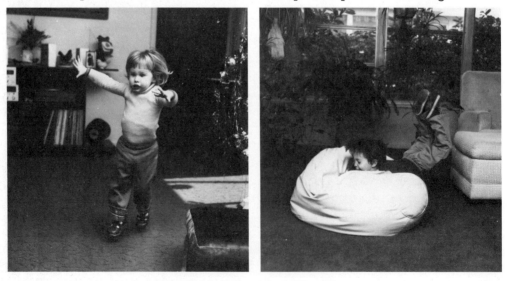

Running and jumping go together. Between two and three years of age, children learn to put a little hop, skip, or jump into their running. When we say "little," we do not exaggerate. Running and jumping over a sock, or over the hose, is considered quite an accomplishment.

Jumping with the aid of a spring is a different matter. Heather demonstrated for us the typical exuberance with which a two-year old rides a rocking horse. The higher the bounce, the better the ride. Similar creatures are available in many parks, and children can be observed wrenching them this way and that, trying to get as much spring as possible. For those who do not have an exotic beast at hand, there always is a bed that can be jumped on. Two year old children have so much fun learning to jump that many parents allow a limited amount of this jumping, at least until the children get bigger and heavier.

Jumping down is another popular pastime. Two-year olds do not have enough strength to jump up very far, but they do have the nerve to jump down, especially if a soft landing is provided for them. We watched Chris and Michael jumping off a coffee table onto a cushion on the floor. The first jump was approached with trepidation, but after that they jumped with the abandon of experienced paratroopers.

Two-year olds continue to develop their climbing skills but there are large differences between individual children. Some children become fearful of heights, while others demonstrate a new strength and agility in their climbing. Brian showed us how he climbed up on the bar to watch the fish. Matthew was one of several children who enjoyed climbing in and out of a crib.

Climbing outside was more difficult. The bars on jungle gyms seemed too

far apart for most two-year olds and the drop to the bottom too great a fall. Jason, who was a talented climber, was willing to try a jungle gym only when his mother was nearby to catch him. Climbing a tree presented similar difficulties. Matthew enjoyed the view but required assistance getting up and down. Climbing a ladder on a slide, or scaling a chain link fence, were more satisfactory challenges for the two-year olds we visited.

Throwing is a body movement that often develops dramatically between two and three. Toddlers flip objects more than they throw them. They do not get their bodies behind the throw and there is only a slight ability to aim. The object may be released too early and fall behind the child. If not, it is likely to go flying off at almost any angle. By the age of three, however, children can aim their throws, although they may choose to tease an adult by throwing a ball in the wrong direction. Because of their greater ability to throw, two-year olds like to play with small balls that can be grasped in one hand. This is in contrast to the preference of toddlers for large balls that can be lugged around.

Small balls are for throwing, large ones are for catching. Billy was able to catch a volleyball by trapping it against his body. This ability was decidedly limited, though. The ball had to be thrown from a very short distance and it had to hit Billy squarely in the chest. Suzanne, on the other hand, was

able to catch a large balloon with just her hands. The balloon traveled through the air so slowly that she could track its motion and respond accordingly.

Body movements of all kinds are involved in gymnastics. Two-year olds are awed by the gymnastic skills of a five-year old, but their ability to join in is rather limited. Somersaults are practiced diligently and, if someone is available to assist, two-year olds like to stand on their heads. Dancing represents a kind of gymnastics that is more manageable. We watched Angela dance enthusiastically to a "Sesame Street" record. Her dancing was full of vigorous arm and leg movements, quite a change from the restrained bounce of a toddler.

The arm and leg coordination that enables two-year olds to run and jump and dance can be applied to a tricycle. Wheels can replace feet as a means of transportation. This is not an instantaneous process, however. The children do not realize the initial force that is necessary to overcome inertia, and they are not sure when each foot should be pressed down on the pedal. The

first movements are a matter of inches and, as Jason demonstrated for us, they are just as likely to be in a backward as a forward direction. The best practicing surface is one that slopes very slightly downhill. Too steep a hill may lead to catastrophe, while the smallest upgrade will stop a novice cyclist in his tracks. The two-year old who gets too frustrated by the whole process will get off and push. In fact, some children get so good at pushing and steering simultaneously that they do not even attempt to ride. Then one day they begin to pedal and, in a short time, they are riding as if they had been doing it all their lives.

A similar kind of coordination is involved in pumping a swing, but most children take longer to learn that. Perhaps it is because parents are more willing to push a swing than a tricycle. Wherever two-year olds gather it is almost a certainty that, sooner or later, they will be found sitting in swings, being pushed by older persons. At this age, swinging is a relaxing activity that children and parents share, a time for talking and laughing together. At some point in the future the parents will expect their children to do the work themselves but, for the time being, they are happy to play a helping role.

Playgrounds in general are a happy place for two-year olds and their parents. Most of the children have overcome earlier fears of slides or swings. Yet they are not quite ready to join in the rough and tumble play of older children. Parents do not have to stand over the children in fear that they are going to break their necks, but at the same time they are still needed: to push the merry-go-round gently, to catch children at the bottom of a tall slide, to help children get down from a platform. It is a situation in which parents can both relax and participate.

Action Games

There are other ways in which parents and two-year olds share physical activity. Jon initiated wrestling matches by jumping on his father whenever he lay down. When Shawn's mother propped her legs on the coffee table, Shawn used them like a bar for somersaulting to the floor. Jenny and her mother liked to put on a record and intersperse their housework with dancing. This is the most interesting characteristic of physical exploration – it invariably leads to a shared activity.

These shared activities have the qualities of a game. There are no winners or losers; instead, certain unwritten rules define the role each player will take. The rules insure that the game will unfold in a similar way every time it is played. Running leads to chase games. Chase games actually start as soon as children can crawl. By the time children are two years old, chasing may have evolved into a simple version of hide and seek. The children run away and hide, knowing full well that their parents will find them because they always hide in the same place. This spot is likely to be a small space, such as a box, a clothes basket or a space behind the sofa into which the child can just barely squeeze. Chase games may be elaborated verbally with two-year olds. Jason's father, for example sang, "All Around the Mulberry Bush" as he chased Jason. The words were adapted to fit the situation: "All around the living room, Daddy chased Jason; Jason sat down in a chair, and Daddy sat down on him."

Jumping leads to jumping games. Usually the child is the jumper and the parent is the catcher. Whenever Robert saw his father was close enough, he jumped off the bathtub ledge or off the crib railing. There wasn't much his father could do but catch Robert; and so far, his father told us, he has not missed. We suspect he enjoyed catching Robert. Erik requested a jumping game while shopping. Each parent held one of his hands while saying, "Jack be nimble, Jack be quick, Jack jump over the candlestick." On the word "over," Erik jumped as high as he could. At the same time his parents lifted him and he seemed to jump two or three feet in the air.

Throwing leads to games of catch. A favorite version among two-year olds was demonstrated by Robert. Before going to sleep, he threw all his stuffed animals out of the crib while his father tried to catch them. Jason and his mother used a bathtub for their game of catch. While Jason was in the tub, his mother tossed him a ball. Inevitably, Jason missed the ball, but it floated right next to him and was easy to retrieve. Jason flung the wet ball back to his mother, who threw him a high one that made a big splash as it landed.

Running, jumping and throwing—these are the activities that seem to

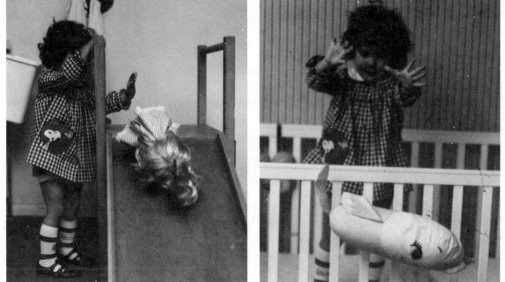

stimulate the greatest number of parent-child play routines. However, we observed other examples. In Matthew's home, father-son wrestling led to a pretend boxing game. Riding a tricycle became a game for Laura when she rode through a tunnel formed by her father's legs. Robert and his parents played a dancing game called "circle" when one of his favorite records was put on the phonograph. Every form of physical activity has the potential of becoming a shared game.

One reason games occur in connection with physical activity is that both children and parents think it is important to develop physical skill. Parents enjoy teaching children how to use their bodies, and they take a great deal of pride in the growing physical ability of their children. This feeling of pride is reflected by the children. Brandon showed us how he could do a somersault. Jodi was proud of being able to stand up in a swing. Daniel was able to jump into a pool and swim back to the side. As he put it, "I make it."

Going Places

As children move their bodies, they learn about the properties of the space around them. Distance takes on more meaning as it comes to be measured in terms of how far one has run, or jumped, or thrown a ball. Relative position becomes understood more fully as children move into, out of, over, under and through other objects.

Most interesting, however, is the two-year old's growing awareness of the way space is organized. Beverly's mother was amazed that Beverly recognized the outside of the hairdresser's shop several months after their visit. This kind of memory for places may be surprising, but it is typical of two-year olds. Children learn to recognize special buildings (such as the doctor's office,) landmarks, or even whole neighborhoods very quickly. Between the ages of two and three, they begin to remember the routes that link these familiar places. Beverly's mother discovered that Beverly would point in the direction the car should go and, more often than not, they would end up at the right place: grandmother's house, the grocery store, the beach.

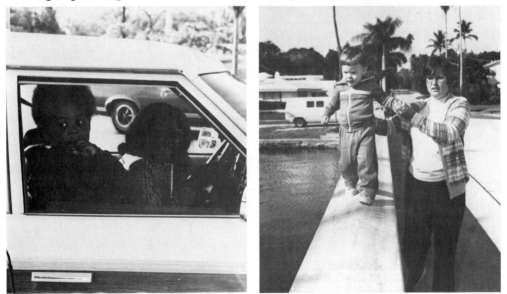

A more intense kind of exploration occurs when two year old children investigate the spatial layout of their immediate environment. They have long been familiar with the organization of their own home, although some new places may be discovered, such as the back of a clothes closet or the space behind the furnace. The space right outside the house is more of an un-known quantity. Two-year olds who are lucky enough to have a fenced-in yard can go out and explore this territory at their leisure. They can closely scru-tinize such details as the mud puddle under the drainpipe, the pile of bricks under the apple tree, and the garbage can near the fence. Two years of age is a good time for really getting to know the backyard and, as Shawn's mother pointed out, it can have a calming influence. Shawn was less restless in-side the house after they moved to a new house with a yard.

Whether or not two year old children have a yard, many of them get a strong urge to wander beyond immediate boundaries. We watched Kim scale a five foot fence in order to chase a duck. Benjie and Jamie liked to visit the neigh-bor next door (although her cat did not like to visit their dog.) Brian had vis-ited the lady across the back fence and now was starting to go down the block. It seems especially nice for two-year olds to have this kind of relationship with neighbors. However, most of the parents in our study were concerned about their children wandering alone at this age. There were dangers the children did not appreciate and there was the possibility of getting lost. Compromises were common: children were allowed to ride their tricycles along the sidewalk in front of the house, but no further. They could visit the next door neighbor, but no further.

By far the most satisfactory compromise, from a child's point of view, takes place when parents agree to accompany children. We wandered along with B.J. and his mother on a walk around the block. During the walk, B.J. was constantly exploring. Some of the things he found interesting were things that appeal to adults as well. He stopped to pet a neighbor's dog, picked some wildflowers, and rolled a few smooth stones around in his hand. Other stops showed the special worldview of a two-year old. At one point he cir-cled a big tree and at another point he tried climbing a fire hydrant. The walk had no definite destination and was not confined to the sidewalk. B.J. strayed onto lawns and walked along ledges. His mother stayed nearby, re-minding him of dangers, talking about the sights, and lending a helping hand when necessary. On the way back, he needed even more than a helping hand so his mother gave him a piggy back ride.

Exploring space is a leisurely process for two year old children. B.J.'s walk was a success because he set the pace. Other families have described to us how unsuccessful walks can be when parents define the goals. Mat-thew's father was looking forward to hiking during a family vacation to the mountains, but the vacation was a disaster. Matthew was not interested in keeping a steady pace in order to look down into a valley, or to admire a wa-terfall. He thought it was a much better idea to meander along the path, stop-ping to chase a butterfly or throw a twig in the stream. As a result, hiking became a hassle. The best part of the vacation, according to Matthew's father, was wandering around every evening looking for firewood and then building a campfire. That was the kind of hiking that made sense to Matthew.

Watching B.J. on his walk, we saw a kind of playful experimentation. With each new object, B.J. seemed to be wondering, what can I do to this, what can this do to me? We have emphasized the two-year old's desire to master skills through exploration, but children at this age are still expert experimenters, especially when exploring something new. They twist, pull, poke, tap, drop, throw and even taste objects, just to see what will happen.

For many two-year olds, the outdoors represents a new and exciting environment for experimentation. Stores, especially large department stores, offer similar possibilites. No longer so overwhelmed by the hustle and bustle of shoppers, or by the staggering array of merchandise, two year old children become more active in stores. They play with items on the shelves, hide under the clothes racks and wander into the changing rooms. The children are interested in learning the layout of the store. In their independent jaunts, they venture further and further from parents and may set off intentionally to investigate another department.

Again, this kind of exploration can be enjoyable for both parents and children if there is plenty of time, enough time to talk to children about what they are discovering and to discuss the limitations of exploration in a store. Playing with a three panel mirror or riding the escalator may be the highlight of the day. Unfortunately, shopping is often a hurried project in which the child's instinct for exploration must be subordinated to the parent's need to finish quickly.

*　　　*　　　*

Through exploration, two-year olds develop skill in using their bodies while gaining a greater understanding of the world in which they live. They learn about the nature of various materials and objects, how they can be combined, taken apart, or restructured into new forms. Above and beyond this information about specific objects, the children develop some broad principles for organizing the world. Most two-year olds in our culture live in an urban environment and their organizing concepts are therefore related to the idea of a city.

First, there is the notion of work done outside the home. The children realize that one or both parents go to a certain place and work. The nature of the work may be a mystery, but the children are often aware that money is associated with work. They also begin to see that different people perform different kinds of work. Of special interest are the workers with uniforms or special hats: policemen, bus drivers, garbage men, barbers, construction workers.

A second idea involves buying and selling. Most prominent is the fact that food is bought at a grocery store. Children also learn at an early age that gas is bought at a service station. Gradually this idea expands, as the children begin to distinguish the separate functions of drug stores, hardware stores, toy stores, and so on. Some department stores carry almost everything, while other stores have only one kind of thing.

A third concept is the idea of private ownership: nearly everything belongs to someone. This is a hard lesson to learn. The things in stores belong to the store until they are bought. The cars in the street belong to different people and cannot be entered at will. Even the grass along the sidewalk is the property of someone else and must be trod on carefully.

These ideas, and others like them, are not generated by any one kind of experience. They are the cumulative result of exploration of all kinds. Between the ages of two and three, these ideas are still vague and are not connected into any consistent system of thought. They are significant, though, because they indicate that the children are becoming aware of the economic and technological structure of our culture. The city is becoming a natural and predictable environment in their eyes.

The importance of parents in guiding and fostering exploration has been implicit throughout this chapter. Although two year old children try to conduct some of their exploration in secret, they typically want parents to pay attention to their activity and to talk with them about it. It is even better if the parents participate in the exploration as well. As Christopher's father told us, "Chris is happy to play with his toys as long as I play along, but if I don't pay attention to him, he will tear the place up."

Involvement with children through exploration gives parents a chance to warn their children of dangers and to explain restrictions. It also gives parents the opportunity to introduce new ideas. Exploration is not always a discovery experience. Parents can suggest a strategy for completing a puzzle, demonstrate a new way of building, or invent an action game. As long as they are not made to feel inferior, two year old children are eager for new ideas. The ultimate goal remains mastery and children look to their parents to help them reach this goal.

SUGGESTED READINGS

For Children

Berenstain, Stan and Jan. *The Berenstain Bears Go to the Doctor* (New York: Random House, 1981).

Berger, Barbara. *Grandfather Twilight* (New York: Philomel Books, 1984).

Brown, Margaret Wise. *The Runaway Bunny* (New York: Harper & Row, 1972).

————. *Where Have You Been?* (New York: Hastings House, 1981).

Burton, Virginia Lee. *Mike Mulligan and His Steam Shovel* (Boston, Massachusetts: Houghton-Mifflin Co., 1939).

Curry, Peter. *Peter Curry's Colors* (Los Angeles, California: Price/Stern/Sloan Publishers, Inc., 1981).

————. *Peter Curry's 1-2-3* (Los Angeles, California: Price/Stern/Sloan Publishers, Inc., 1981).

————. *My Favorite Thing* (New York: Grosset & Dunlap, 1978).

Fujikawa, Gyo. *Betty Bear's Birthday Party* (New York: Grosset & Dunlap, 1977).

Kessler, Ethel and Leonard. *Splish, Splash!* (New York: Scholastic, 1973).

Kingsley, Emily Perl. *I Can Do It Myself* (Racine, Wisconsin: Western Publishing Company, Inc., 1980).

Koelling, Caryl. *A Surprise For Your Eyes* (Los Angeles, California: Intervisual Communications, Inc., 1981).

Long, Earlene. *Johnny's Egg* (Reading, Massachusetts: Addison-Wesley, 1980).

Nedobeck's Numbers Book (Milwaukee, Wisconsin: Ideal Publishing Co., 1981).

Rice, Eve. *Goodnight, Goodnight* (New York: Greenwillow Books, 1980).

Roberts, Sarah. *Don't Cry, Big Bird* (New York: Random House, 1981).

Dr. Seuss. *The Cat In the Hat* (New York: Random House, 1957).

Watanabe, Shigeo. *How Do I Put It On?* (New York: Philomel Books, 1977).

For Parents

Brazelton, T. Berry. *Toddlers and Parents* (New York: Delacorte Press/Seymour Lawrence, 1974).

————. *To Listen to a Child* (Reading, Massachusetts: Addison-Wesley, 1984).

Cass-Beggs, Barbara. *Your Baby Needs Music* (New York: St. Martin's Press, 1978).

Church, Joseph. *Understanding Your Child From Birth to Three* (New York: Pocket Books, 1976).

Cole, Ann Hass; Bushnell, Carolyn; Weinberger, Frank and Betty. *Saw a Purple Cow and 100 Other Recipes for Learning* (Boston; Massachusetts: Little, Brown and Company, 1972).

Forman, George E. and Kuschner, David S. *The Child's Construction Of Knowledge* (Washington, D. C.: National Association for Education of Young Children, 1983).

Gordon, Ira J.; Guinach, Barry; and Jester, R. Emile. *Child Learning Through Child Play* (New York: St. Martin's Press, 1972).

Rovee-Collier, Carolyn, ed. *Infant Behavior And Development,* Volume 7, Number 4, October–December 1984 (Norwood, New Jersey: Ablex Publishing Corp., 1984).

Singer, D., and Singer, G. *Partners In Play* (New York: Harper and Row, 1977).

Sulton-Smith, B. *How to Play With Your Children* (New York: Hawthorn Press, 1974).

INDEX

Keeping Up With Your Toddler . . .

It's fun to keep track of what your toddler does. On these pages list some of the things you notice about your toddler—his or her personality, favorite toys and activities, new accomplishments, family events.

Keeping Up With Your Toddler . . .

Keeping Up With Your Toddler . . .

Keeping Up With Your Toddler . . .

Keeping Up With Your Toddler . . .

Keeping Up With Your Toddler . . .

Keeping Up With Your Toddler . . .

Keeping Up With Your Toddler . . .

About the Authors

Marilyn Segal, Ph.D., a developmental psychologist specializing in early childhood, is professor of human development and director of the Family Center at Nova University in Fort Lauderdale, Florida. The mother of five children, she is the author of sixteen books, including *Making Friends, Just Pretending,* and the three-volume series *Your Child at Play.* She is also the creator of the nine-part television series "To Reach a Child."

Don Adcock, Ph.D., is an associate director of the Family Center, a developmental psychologist, and a professor of early childhood development at Metropolitan State Hospital in Denver, Colorado. He is the coauthor of several books with Dr. Segal.

Parenting and Child Care Books Available from Newmarket Press

Baby Massage
Parent-Child Bonding Through Touching
by Amelia D. Auckett; introduction by Eva Reich, M.D.

Here is a fully-illustrated, practical, time-tested approach to baby massage; an invaluable book for all those concerned with the care and nurturing of infants. Topics include: bonding and body contact; baby massage as an alternative to drugs; healing the effects of birth trauma; baby massage as an expression of love.

(128 pages, 34 photos and drawings; bibliography, index; 5½ × 8¼"; ISBN 0-937858-07-2; $6.95, paperback)

What's Happening to My Body?
A Growing Up Guide for Parents and Daughters
by Lynda Madaras, with Area Madaras; forewords by Ralph I. Lopez, M.D., and Cynthia W. Cooke, M.D.

This carefully researched book provides detailed explanations of what takes place in a girl's body as she grows up, and includes chapters on: changing size and shape; changes in the reproductive organs; menstruation; puberty in boys; and much more. Named a "Best Book for Young Adults, 1983" by the American Library Association.
(208 pages, 42 drawings, charts, and diagrams; bibliography, index; 5½ × 8¼"; ISBN 0-937858-25-0, $14.95, hardcover; ISBN 0-937858-21-8, $8.95, paperback)

The "What's Happening to My Body?" Book for Boys
A Growing Up Guide for Parents and Sons
by Lynda Madaras, with Dane Saavedra; foreword by Ralph I. Lopez, M.D.

Like her puberty book for girls, Madaras' new book for parents and their sons is written in a comfortable, non-judgmental tone and will help boys understand the changes that are, or soon will be, taking place in their body. Chapters include: changing size and shape; hair, perspiration, pimples, and voice changes; sexuality; and much more.
(240 pages, 40 drawings; bibliography, index; 5½ × 8¼"; ISBN 0-937858-39-0, $14.95, hardcover; ISBN 0-937858-40-4, $8.95, paperback)

(continued on next page)

And the three-volume series of books that enhance communication between parent and child—"Insightful, warm, and practical . . . expert knowledge that's a must for every parent." (T. Berry Brazelton)

Your Child at Play: Birth to One Year
Discovering the Senses and Learning About the World
by Marilyn Segal, Ph.D.

Playing with your child is much more than fun and games—it's a vital part of your child's intellectual, emotional, social, and physical development. In *Your Child at Play: Birth to One Year*, Dr. Marilyn Segal brings you into your baby's world, discussing the subtle developmental changes that take place in each of the first twelve months of life, and presenting hundreds of games and activities that parent and child can enjoy together during day-to-day routines.
(288 pages, 250 photos; bibliography; 7¼ × 9"; ISBN 0-937858-50-1, $14.95, hardcover; ISBN 0-937858-51-X, $8.95, paperback)

Your Child at Play: One to Two Years
Exploring, Daily Living, Learning, and Making Friends
by Marilyn Segal, Ph.D., and Don Adcock, Ph.D.

A vivid look at everyday life with a toddler, *Your Child at Play: One to Two Years* is filled with hundreds of practical suggestions for creative play activities, managing problem situations, and making the most of the growth spurt that takes place during this year. Because toddlers have such different rates and patterns of development, the book is organized by topic rather than by month. It is fully illustrated and features anecdotes and descriptions of one- to two-year olds that every parent will recognize and appreciate.
(244 pages, 300 photos; bibliography, index; 7¼ × 9"; ISBN 0-937858-52-8, $14.95, hardcover; ISBN 0-937858-53-6, $8.95, paperback)

Your Child at Play: Two to Three Years
Growing Up, Language, and the Imagination
by Marilyn Segal, Ph.D., and Don Adcock, Ph.D.

Two-year olds progress at such a rapid rate that it often leaves their families dazzled and a bit confused. *Your Child at Play: Two to Three Years* provides a vivid description of how two-year olds see themselves; how they get along with others and make friends; and how they learn language, begin to play imaginatively, and continue exploring their surroundings. The book is fully illustrated and filled with hundreds of innovative ideas for games and activities that parent and child can enjoy together.
(208 pages, 200 photos; bibliography, index; 7¼ × 9"; ISBN 0-937858-54-4, $14.95, hardcover; ISBN 0-937858-55-2, $8.95, paperback)

Ask for these titles at your local bookstore or
order today

Use this coupon or write to: NEWMARKET PRESS, 3 East 48th Street, New York, NY 10017

Please send me:

_____copies of BABY MASSAGE @ $6.95 (trade paperback) ISBN 0-937858-07-2

_____copies of WHAT'S HAPPENING TO MY BODY? @ $14.95 (hardcover) ISBN 0-937858-25-0

_____copies of WHAT'S HAPPENING TO MY BODY @ $8.95 (trade paperback) ISBN 0-937858-21-8

_____copies of THE "WHAT'S HAPPENING TO MY BODY?" BOOK FOR BOYS @ $14.95 (hardcover) ISBN 0-937858-39-0

_____copies of THE "WHAT'S HAPPENING TO MY BODY?" BOOK FOR BOYS @ $8.95 (trade paperback) ISBN 0-937858-40-4

_____copies of YOUR CHILD AT PLAY: BIRTH TO ONE YEAR @ $14.95 (hardcover) ISBN 0-937858-50-1

_____copies of YOUR CHILD AT PLAY: BIRTH TO ONE YEAR @ $8.95 (trade paperback) ISBN 0-937858-51-X

_____copies of YOUR CHILD AT PLAY: ONE TO TWO YEARS @ $14.95 (hardcover) ISBN 0-937858-52-8

_____copies of YOUR CHILD AT PLAY: ONE TO TWO YEARS @ $8.95 (trade paperback) ISBN 0-937858-53-6

_____copies of YOUR CHILD AT PLAY: TWO TO THREE YEARS @ $14.95 (hardcover) ISBN 0-937858-54-4

_____copies of YOUR CHILD AT PLAY: TWO TO THREE YEARS @ $8.95 (trade paperback) ISBN 0-937858-55-2

Add $1.50 per order for postage and handling. Allow 4-6 weeks for delivery. (NY resident, please add applicable state and local sales tax.)

I enclose a check or money order payable to NEWMARKET PRESS in the amount of $_____.

NAME_____

ADDRESS_____

CITY/STATE/ZIP_____

For quotes on quantity purchases, or for a free copy of our catalog, please write or phone Newmarket Press, 3 East 48th Street, New York, NY 10017. 212-832-3575.